M000291337

WHO KNOWS?

WHO KNOWS?

A Study of Religious Consciousness

Raymond M. Smullyan

INDIANA
University Press

Bloomington & Indianapolis

This book is a publication of

Indiana University Press
601 North Morton Street
Bloomington, Indiana 47404-3797 USA

http://iupress.indiana.edu

Telephone orders   800-842-6796
Fax orders   812-855-7931
Orders by e-mail   iuporder@indiana.edu

Manufactured in the United States of America

Library of Congress Cataloging-in-Publication Data

Smullyan, Raymond M.
  Who knows? : a study of religious consciousness / Raymond Smullyan.
    p. cm.
Includes bibliographical references and index.
  ISBN 0-253-34198-1 (alk. paper) — ISBN 0-253-21574-9 (pbk. : alk.
paper)
  1. Religion. 2. Hell. 3. Future life. 4. God. 5. Christianity. 6.
Gardner, Martin, 1914– Whys of a philosophical scrivener. 7. Bucke,
Richard Maurice, 1837–1902. Cosmic consciousness. I. Title.
  BL50 .S59 2003
  210—dc21
                              2002008868

1 2 3 4 5 08 07 06 05 04 03

I believe all religions are true.
—*Walt Whitman*

I believe no religions are true.
—*Anonymous*

CONTENTS

PREFACE

Is there really a God, and if so, what is He (She? It?) actually like? Is there really an afterlife, or is the belief in one mere superstitious, primitive, childish, wishful thinking? Is there actually one scrap of scientific evidence either for or against the possibility or probability of an afterlife? And if there is an afterlife, is there really such a thing as eternal punishment for unrepentant sinners, as many orthodox Christians and Moslems believe? And if there is, is God unwilling or unable to relieve the sufferings of those in Hell? Is it true, as St. Augustine said, that God could save *everyone*, if He wanted to, and the reason He doesn't is that He will not? Could a kind God really allow such a horrible thing as Hell, or is the belief that it is horrible due to the fallen nature of Man, as some orthodox religionists claim? After all, there are those like Jonathan Edwards who found the idea of Hell, not horrible, but beautiful! (Before his conversion, he found it horrible, but after his conversion, he found it "sweet.")

Next, what about mystics; are they in possession of some higher knowledge, or are they simply fooling themselves? Is it really true that our unconscious minds are connected to a higher spiritual reality, as believed by those like William James, and if so, could this higher spiritual reality be the very same thing that religionists call *God?* And what about the remarkable idea advanced by those like Richard Bucke and Edward Carpenter, that through the process of evolution, the human race is developing a higher type of consciousness called *Cosmic Consciousness,* which will ultimately enable us to directly perceive that which hitherto was believed merely on faith? Beautiful and optimistic as is this idea, is it a reality or merely a pleasant pipe dream?

These are some of the questions addressed in this book. Surely, it is helpful to consider the strongest possible arguments both for and against any theological or philosophical position, and this is what I have tried to do with many of the questions concerned. Martin Gardner—a famous writer on mathematical games and puzzles—has written a book, *The Whys of a Philosophical Scrivener,* in which many chapters are devoted to theological topics. Part I of my book is a commentary on these chapters. Part II is exclusively on the doctrine of Hell, in which I consider the strongest arguments for and against that I know, and conclude that the idea is logically consistent and hopefully false. From these dark clouds, we pass in Part III to the sunshine of Cosmic Consciousness—a sublime subject that deserves to be far better known than it apparently is these days.

I wish to express my thanks to my wife Blanche and my friends George and Matina Billias for their helpful interest in the progress of this work. Especial thanks are due to Professor James Hart of the Department of Religious Studies at Indiana University, whose encouragement and suggestions have been invaluable.

Elka Park, New York

WHO KNOWS?

I Wherefore the Whys

For just as it is always possible to ask the why of every why so it is possible to ask the wherefore of every wherefore.

—*Miguel de Unamuno*

Wherefore the Whys of a Philosophical Scrivener?

Martin Gardner has left us a host of thought-provoking thoughts on religion (as well as other topics) in his book *The Whys of a Philosophical Scrivener,* and I would like to share some of my own thoughts that his have provoked. This will be far more than a mere review, since I will ramble freely back and forth as my fancy carries me, exploring many byways and side paths, but hopefully returning to the main path from time to time. After all, Gardner himself somewhere in his book describes it as "rambling" (which fortunately it is, in a very delightful and instructive way), so why shouldn't I follow suit?

In a conversation about religion that I once had with a mathematician and an ex-Catholic, he said, "Suppose someone proved to my satisfaction that there is a God. I would reply, 'So what?'" How very different Gardner's attitude is, as expressed toward the beginning of chapter 10, in which he says, "It has been said that all philosophers can be divided into two categories: those who divide philosophers into two categories and those who don't. I belong to the first. I believe that the dichotomy between those who believe in a creator God and those who do not is the deepest, most fundamental of all divisions among the attitudes one can take toward the mystery of being" (Gardner 1983, p. 168).

Now for my first ramble: I agree that the difference between belief in God and nonbelief may be of some importance, but I can think of far more important differences. For one thing, I have always felt that the gap between atheism and belief in God is extremely small compared with the difference between a mere belief that there is a God *and the belief that God wrote any of the existing holy books!* A mere belief in a creator God, without postulating any properties to this God, would hardly have much effect on how one would conduct one's life, whereas any of the orthodox religions are chock full of moral regulations. Stated otherwise, the gap between atheism and natural religion is small compared to that between natural religion and revealed religion. (Curiously enough, though, with many of the eighteenth-century English and Continental deists, their concept of God was highly influenced by many ideas of the Judeo-Christian tradition.)

Let me put the matter another way: I would say that whether or not one believes in God is less important—far less important—than the kind of God in whom one believes. As a drastic example (and I can't think of a more drastic one), just compare a Christian Universalist, or equally, an orthodox Buddhist or Hindu, who believes that all souls ultimately obtain salvation, with a Christian or Moslem who believes that some (if not most) souls are destined for eternal torment in hell. (Incidentally, in a letter to Martin Gardner, I asked him whether, despite his belief in God, he doesn't feel closer to the atheist than to the one who believes both in God and in eternal punishment. He assured me that of the two, he prefers the atheist. Gardner shares my utter abhorrence of the doctrine of eternal punishment, thank God!) Indeed, I might well go so far as to say that I regard *the* most important difference of all to be between those who believe in and condone eternal punishment and those who do not. (Please note carefully that I added "and condone." It is one thing to believe in eternal punishment out of fear that if one doesn't, one will be eternally punished, and quite another thing to approve of it! But then again, one might out of fear hypnotize oneself into approving of it, so perhaps the two are not so different after all! But more of this in Part II of this book.)

Many readers of Gardner's book who regard the existence of God and the afterlife to be sheer superstitions of the same caliber as beliefs in astrology, witchcraft, clairvoyance, extrasensory perception, and other occultisms have been quite shocked that Martin Gardner—a lifelong crusader against paranormal science—should actually believe in God and an afterlife!

Should these two beliefs be classified as superstitions? Well, of course, there is the logical possibility that both beliefs are true, in which case, could they be superstitions? More generally, is it possible to have a superstitious belief in a true proposition? Suppose, for example, that one believes a proposition for which one has no evidence, but the proposition (by luck) happens to be true. Should the belief then be called a superstition? Perhaps the answer depends on the nature of the belief. For example, suppose it actually turns out that, for some unknown reason, thirteen is really an unlucky number. Should the belief that it is then be regarded as a superstition? I would say that it should, since the believer had no way of *knowing* that it was true. On the other hand, suppose there really is a God who influences some people to believe in Him by some means we do not understand. Then I would hardly regard the belief of those so influenced as a superstition—even though they had no objective evidence for the belief. But it is also possible that there is a God who does *not* influence anyone to believe in Him—the beliefs of those who do may be totally unrelated to the actuality of His existence—the believers have simply made lucky guesses. In that case, should their beliefs be called superstitious? That's a hard question to answer.

So far, we have considered only the case that there is a God; now suppose there isn't? Is the belief in God then necessarily a superstition? I tend to doubt it. There are many people who believe that there is absolutely no evidence either for or against the existence of God. I tend rather to an opposite opinion—namely, that there is some evidence both for and against the existence of God! Neither evidence is compelling; both are circumstantial. Let me explain.

The argument from design—generally in disfavor these days, even by some believers—has, I believe, *some* merit. It certainly does not qualify as a *proof*, but does constitute some degree of what might aptly be called *circumstantial evidence*. It is my firm belief that any completely unbiased person, seeing the wonder around us, would come to the conclusion, not that it *must* have been planned, but that it more likely has been planned than not. And this is what I call circumstantial evidence on the positive side. On the negative side, I certainly regard the fact that God does not communicate with us in a generally recognizable fashion, plus the sufferings and evils of the world, as very strong evidence against a God—certainly an all-powerful and all-good one, as many define God to be. Yes, I am familiar with many of the arguments of the theologians explaining the problem of evil, and I grant that none of these arguments are positively *disprovable*. (It is *logically* possible that all our sufferings are good for us in the long run for reasons we don't understand.) Nevertheless, I believe that any impartial person would find these arguments to be extremely contrived and implausible—

he would find it, not impossible, but implausible that a perfect being would create an imperfect world. Thus, on the one hand, the remarkable design of the world suggests a planner, but the imperfection of the world virtually rules out a *perfect* planner. I would thus say that the weight of evidence points to an *evolving* Deity—one who is not yet perfect—but I'll have more to say about that later.

Now, to Martin Gardner, *evidence* for the existence of God is not the really important thing. Indeed, he devotes a whole chapter to explaining why he believes that God's existence cannot be demonstrated. His belief in God is admittedly one of pure faith, and he makes the leap of faith for two reasons: (1) he wants a God to whom he can pray for forgiveness of his sins; and (2) he wants a God who is sufficiently powerful and merciful to grant us immortality. He, like Miguel de Unamuno, whom he greatly admires, is honest enough to admit that he believes in God and immortality because he *wants* these things to be true. As he well puts it in his chapter on faith: "I am quite content to confess with Unamuno that I have no basis whatever for my belief in God other than a passionate longing that God exists and that I and others will not cease to exist" (p. 222).

Personally, I find this honesty most admirable! Here I totally disagree with Bertrand Russell, for whom I usually have the greatest admiration. Russell (an avowed atheist and rationalist) stated in his *A History of Western Philosophy* that he prefers someone like Thomas Aquinas, who at least *attempts* a rational approach to God's existence, to someone like Rousseau, who is willing to accept God's existence without any pretense of rational arguments whatsoever. Russell believes that Aquinas's approach is the more honest. Here is the exact quote:

> For my part, I prefer the ontological argument, the cosmological argument, and the rest of the old stock-in-trade to the sentimental illogicality that has sprung from Rousseau. The old arguments were at least honest: if invalid, it was open to any critic to prove them so. But the new theology of the heart dispenses with arguments; it cannot be refuted, because it does not profess to prove its points. At bottom, the only reason offered for its acceptance is that it allows us to indulge in pleasant dreams. This is an unworthy reason, and if I had to choose between Thomas Aquinas and Rousseau, I should unhesitatingly choose the saint. (Russell 1945, p. 694)

As I said, I completely disagree! I regard the arguments of those like Aquinas to be sheer rationalizations of beliefs whose origins are not known even to the believers themselves. Isn't it more honest to simply say, "I believe. I know not why"? What could be more honest than that? It might be of interest to note that Russell has quite a different attitude elsewhere in the same book. Toward the end of his chapter on Aquinas, after stating some of the merits of his system, he says:

> These merits, however, seem scarcely sufficient to justify his immense reputation. The appeal to reason is, in a sense, insincere, since the conclusion to be reached is fixed in advance. . . . There is little of the true philosophical spirit in Aquinas. . . . He is not engaged in an inquiry, the result of which it is impossible to know in advance. Before he begins to philosophize, he already knows the truth; it is declared in the Catholic faith. If he can find apparently rational arguments for some parts of the faith, so much the better; if he cannot, he need only fall back on revelation. The finding of arguments for a conclusion given in advance is not philosophizing, but special pleading. (pp. 462–63)

And so in this passage, Russell realizes (as do I) that, in many cases, the so-called "rational" approach to religion is nothing more than rationalization. But Russell and I still disagree about beliefs based honestly on pure faith—he condemns them and I do not. Many others condemn beliefs based purely on faith, and I never can quite understand what they mean when they say that one *shouldn't* believe something merely on the basis of faith. Is the word "shouldn't" then to be understood in a moral sense? Or is it meant that a belief based purely on faith is more likely to be wrong than right? If the latter is meant, I sure would love to see a *proof* of the assertion!

Coming back to Martin Gardner, I said I admire him for his honesty in describing his attitude toward God and immortality. I find less admirable his attitude toward atheists and agnostics. In chapter 10 he says:

> Let us not waste time distinguishing the atheists model from the agnostics. It is trivially true that there is no way to prove God's nonexistence. Someone says: "I don't believe in God, but of course I can't be absolutely certain there is no God. Therefore I call myself an agnostic." Is not that person taking a position indistinguishable from the vast majority of thinkers who have called themselves atheists? Is there

any significant difference between not believing in God and believing there is no God, or not believing in an afterlife and believing there is no afterlife? (Gardner 1983, p. 169)

These are good questions and deserve careful and candid answers. Yes, I say there is a *most* significant difference in both cases. Let us first consider atheism and agnosticism with respect to the existence of God. As I see it, both the atheist and the believer are biased in different directions; neither one is really impartial (not that I believe either one necessarily should be!). By contrast, the agnostic takes the most objective, impartial, and purely scientific attitude of all and honestly says, "We don't know." Isn't there something very admirable in this attitude? Now, please understand, I have complete respect for the one who believes in God, if only on the basis of his own feelings which he trusts, and I have equal respect for the atheist who rejects the existence of God on sincere grounds (such as the belief that the available evidence is really against it, or on moral grounds arising from the realization of the horrors that have been perpetrated in the name of religion and the consequent fear that religion is essentially tied up with intolerance). But this should not detract one iota from the respect due to the agnostic for his absolute impartiality. I firmly believe that if there really is a God—and the kind of God I would respect—then God Himself would have equal respect for sincere atheists, sincere agnostics, and sincere believers.

Next, the question of an afterlife: Is there any significant difference between not believing there is one and believing there isn't one? Yes, here I'd say the difference is even more drastic: If one believes that there definitely is no afterlife, then there is no room to even *hope* for one, whereas if a person is undecided on the issue, then he at least has room for hope. Doesn't that constitute a pretty drastic difference?

Coming back to belief in God, I wonder how a person should be classified who thinks as follows: "I have no evidence for or against the existence of God, but I sure *hope* there is one." Should such a person be classified as an atheist or a believer? Another thought— Suppose someone has the following attitude: "Yes, I believe that a creator God exists, but I have no idea what He is like, what He wants me to do; I seem to have no relation to Him whatsoever, and as far as I'm concerned, He could just as well not exist!" Isn't such a person, though technically a believer, more like an atheist—at least in a practical sense?

As a "dual" to this thought, suppose there is a person who seems steeped in religion from head to foot; he is constantly praying, attending religious services, and reading religious literature. His whole life is centered around religion. Someone asks him, "You actually believe that God is a reality?" To the questioner's surprise, he gets the answer "Oh no; I never thought of God as a reality! To me God is an *ideal*. But I believe that an ideal is just as worthy of reverence and devotion as a reality." Should such a person be regarded as an atheist or a believer? I suppose that technically he is an atheist, but in *spirit*, isn't he more like a believer?

I know a very remarkable lady who is a painter, poet, and playwright. She is devoutly religious and calls herself a Christian Buddhist. (She believes that Jesus was a Buddha.) She also takes a most active interest in political matters, and during the Vietnam War was on Nixon's blacklist for refusing to pay income tax. (She reported her exact earnings and computed her income tax and explained that instead of paying it to the government, she would pay it to a peace organization.) She is a Universalist and believes that all souls are ultimately saved, but in many cases only after numerous lifetimes. To my great surprise, she once told me that God exists purely in the mind! (That reminded me of my fantasy that God exists purely as an ideal!) Sometime later, I asked her how her vision differs from atheism. She replied, "Atheists also believe that God exists purely in the mind, but the atheists believe that God is therefore unreal, whereas I believe that things existing in the mind can be real." (Incidentally, this lady has great respect for atheists and once said about them, "I think the atheists have done a *wonderful* job in helping religion!")

I would like to say a word about some people I know whom I would not classify as atheists, believers, or agnostics. They are people who have no thoughts about God at all. God simply doesn't enter their world; they are totally unaware of either any presence or absence of God. One might be tempted to think of them as agnostics, but this doesn't strike me as quite right: Agnosticism has somewhat the character of a philosophical position (it is *unknown*), but the people I am talking about are not philosophizing, they are just simply living. In some way that I cannot explain, these people strike me as the most religious of all!

After this ramble, let me return to Gardner's book. I find it strange that Gardner should so closely identify the question of whether there is a God with the question of whether there is an afterlife. These are really absolutely different questions, and many people seem blind to this fact! Even Kant made a confusion here: In *The Critique of Pure Reason,* he gave arguments why it is impossible to prove the existence of God. Then in *The Critique of Practical Reason* he states that it is nevertheless necessary to postulate God's existence for the following reasons: Kant takes as a morally self-evident premise that absolute justice must ultimately prevail in the universe. (He quite honestly states that if anyone should ask him why he believes this, he would reply that it is simply his nature to do so.) Now, of course, this basic premise is open to question, but let's give him the benefit of the doubt and go along with it for awhile. Then (reasons Kant), since it is obvious that justice does not prevail in this life, there must be a future life in which the victims of our worldly injustice are compensated and the perpetrators punished, and hence there must be a God. Now, the argument is fine (granting that justice must prevail) up to the point of there having to be an afterlife, but why does it then follow that there must be a God? As far as I know, Kant gave no proof that the existence of God is necessary for an afterlife. And so, the most that can be deduced from Kant's fundamental premise is that there is an afterlife, not that there is a God!

As I have said, Martin Gardner tends to regard the two questions as more tied together than I believe is warranted. He says in chapter 13, "I have spoken of God and immortality as twin objects of faith. . . . Following such fideists as Immanuel Kant and Miguel de Unamuno, and in line with the overwhelming majority of theists, past and present, I will assume that the two beliefs go hand in hand and are mutually reinforcing" (p. 211).

I believe that Gardner here is simply wrong! Just because Kant and Unamuno and many theists tie the two together doesn't mean that they *should* be tied together. I know many people who believe that the two issues should be treated separately. True, Gardner does continue:

> Not that they can't be separated. Many thinkers have professed God while denying an afterlife, but in almost every case the God involved is a pantheistic deity. . . .

It is easier, perhaps, to hope for or even believe in an afterlife without faith in a personal God. One simply regards survival as part of the nature of things. . . .

Although it is possible to believe in God without believing in immortality, and vice versa, both views are extremely rare, and in any case they play no role in what follows. (ibid.)

Well, I think they *should* have played more of a role in what follows! Also, I don't believe that those who distinguish between the two questions are as rare as Gardner says. Surely, many Buddhists believe in an afterlife without believing in God. The same goes for many theosophists. And as for Jews and Christians—or at least those who call themselves such—it seems to me that many of them *these days* believe in God but not in an afterlife. In the last hundred years, hasn't the belief in an afterlife declined much farther than belief in God? Martin quotes Unamuno, who tells of suggesting to a peasant that there might be a God who governs heaven and earth, but that we may not be immortal in the traditional sense. The peasant responded, "Then wherefore God?"

I have had a similar experience: A friend of mine who is devoutly atheistic once told me that if there were no such thing as death, then nobody would believe in God. (Personally, I don't believe that for one minute!) I then mentioned the possibility that there may be a God but no afterlife. He replied, "Then why God?" I must say that this reply (like the peasant's reply in the Unamuno story) strikes me as inappropriate for at least two reasons: First of all, isn't it possible that God's existence is necessary for us to have even *this* life? Second, and perhaps more importantly, why take such an anthropocentric view of God's raison d'être, as if His only purpose is to serve *us*?

I once told a Jehovah's Witness (who was, of course, trying to convert me) that I personally had a much stronger belief in an afterlife than in the existence of God.

He asked, "How can there be an afterlife without God?"

I replied, "Why *can't* there be an afterlife without God?" I then hastened to explain what I had in mind, which is this: In general, I am very disturbed by questions of the form, How can there be a *this* without a *that?* What bothers me is that I usually cannot understand the meaning of "How can there be?" in this connection, since I see no reason why there can't be. For example, I once told a materialist that I see no reason why there cannot be disembodied spirits—why can't there be minds without bodies.

He replied, "How can there be a mind without a body?"

I replied, "Why can't there be?" and we could never get beyond this impasse. (Of course, the *correct* way beyond such an impasse is to realize that when someone says that he sees no reason why something should not be possible, it is not incumbent on him to explain *how* it is possible, but if someone says that something is *impossible,* then it is incumbent on him to prove that it is impossible —it is not enough for him to merely say, "How could it be possible?")

Coming back to the Jehovah's Witness, I continued by explaining that if someone says that God is necessary for *everything,* then although I do not necessarily agree, I can see *some* possible truth in it. But the idea that God is not necessary for this life but is necessary for the next life strikes me as preposterous! (To digress for a moment, the Jehovah's Witness asked me what it would take for me to definitely believe in a personal God. I told him that certainly no *argument* could convince me, since I have heard pretty much all arguments for and against the existence of God, and not one of them did I find convincing, but that the only way I could believe in a personal God is that some internal change would take place in my psyche. This, I assured him—to make him happy—was not impossible.)

Coming back to Gardner's book, I recently had the following thought: Gardner says in chapter 13 that a personal God who did not provide for immortality would be a God less just and merciful than you and I. I can see one way in which this could be false— namely, that it may be possible that much as we may *desire* an afterlife, having one would not be *good* for us (for some reason we don't understand), hence God in his mercy sees to it that we *don't* have an afterlife! Maybe that's the true function (from our point of view) of an all-powerful and merciful God—to prevent us from having that which we desire, but which is bad for us. This then would constitute another possible answer to the question "If no immortality, then why God?" (Incidentally, I told this idea to Gardner, who had a good laugh and said, "That sounds like pure Smullyan!" Actually, I don't believe this idea for one moment, but l am amused at the thought that it is at least possible.)

Next, in chapter 11, Gardner explains why he is not a pantheist. Toward the very beginning, he says that it is not easy to pray to a pantheistic deity, and it is not easy for a pantheist to hope for immortality. I agree with the first, but I believe the second to be absolutely wrong! My reasons are the same as those I have already indicated: I do not positively disbelieve in a personal God (though I prefer a more pantheistic model), but no one has ever yet given me the slightest reason to believe that any kind of God—personal or otherwise—is the least bit necessary for an afterlife. I can personally testify that even in my most pantheistic moods (and, frankly, my religious moods vary enormously from time to time) I believe in an afterlife just as strongly as when I am in a more orthodox religious mood (which also happens to me at times, unfortunately!). Of course, I am only one person, but I know many others who are close to some form of pantheism and who believe in an afterlife.

I will digress again. I wish to say a little about my belief in an afterlife in comparison with that of Martin Gardner. When I have told people of my belief in an afterlife, I have been often asked, "What evidence do you have?" My constant reply is "Absolutely none whatsoever." I don't believe there is the slightest evidence for or against an afterlife. (Here I differ from Gardner, who has privately told me that he believes that the objective evidence is slightly *against* an afterlife. The lack of positive evidence—he believes—constitutes a small degree of negative evidence. I will discuss later why I disagree with this.)

"Then," people ask me, "why *do* you believe in an afterlife?"

"I have no idea *why*," I reply. "I just simply *do*."

"Ah, wishful thinking!" is the standard response.

Well, now, let us see!

The following three propositions are certainly true: (1) I prefer that we have afterlives than that we don't, (2) I believe that we do, (3) I have not the slightest evidence to support my belief (nor any against it). From (1), (2), and (3), a *natural* conclusion to be drawn is that (1) is the *cause* of (2)—my *desire* for an afterlife is the true reason—the true *cause* of my belief that there is one. Natural as this conclusion may be, I ask whether it is valid! What proof is there that when a person believes something that he *wants* to be true and for which he has no evidence, the *only* explanation is wishful thinking? Now, I grant that, in certain cases, this *may* be the correct explanation, but to insist that in all such cases it is the *only* explanation—what warrant is there for this? One might reply, "Well, what other explanation could there be?" I find that an inadequate reply, since it is perfectly possible that the true cause of the belief may be unknown. (I believe that all of us have many beliefs, the real causes of which are not known, despite the many smart alecks who *think* they know the causes!)

It is nevertheless of interest to consider what other possible causes than wishful thinking there could be for someone to believe in an afterlife without evidence. Of course, there is the supernatural possibility that there really is a personal God who directly influences some people to believe in an afterlife (the influence may come through the subconscious), and that would be the end of the matter. I, for one, do not completely rule this out. Even without a God, there may be some other supernatural explanation—supernatural in the sense of going beyond the known laws of science, but not necessarily in opposition to them. (I am thinking of something like the growth of Cosmic Consciousness within one, which I will discuss in the third part of this book.) For the reader who has no patience with anything smacking of the "supernatural," is there any possible *natural* cause other than wishful thinking for the rationally unwarranted belief in an afterlife?

I think a very valuable clue here has been provided by Sigmund Freud in a passage I stumbled across and which appears to be very little known. Of course, Freud was a militant atheist and certainly disbelieved in any possibility of an afterlife. Nevertheless, in his 1915 paper *Thoughts for the Times on War and Death* in part II (titled "Our Attitude towards Death") he says, "Our own death is indeed unimaginable, and whenever we make the attempt to imagine it, we can perceive that we really survive as spectators. Hence, the psychoanalytic school could venture on the assertion that at the bottom no one believes in his own death, or to put the same thing in another way, in the unconscious, everyone is convinced of his own immortality" (Freud 1958, 222–23). What wise words! And what an amazing amount of incredibility and anxiety they have produced on many a nonbeliever in immortality to whom I have told them! Many of them (who in other respects are strongly pro-Freudian) have angrily explained, "I don't believe it! Maybe other people unconsciously believe in an afterlife, but I'm sure *I* don't!" Of course, Freud has never *proved* his point, but it strikes me as thoroughly reasonable and provides the best explanation I can think of as to why many people believe in an afterlife even without rational evidence—namely, in such people, their conscious minds are particularly close to their subconscious ones. Again, I cannot *prove* this; all I can say is that it strikes me as the most plausible explanation I know.

I believe that Goethe somewhere said that the reason for his believing in an afterlife was that he simply could not conceive of himself as not existing, and he could hardly believe something that he could not even imagine! And so Goethe on a *conscious* level reacted exactly as Freud says that all of us react on an unconscious level. I have known others who have reacted similarly on a purely conscious level—I am one such person. I believe that my inability to conceive of myself as nonexisting is a far more potent factor in my belief in an afterlife than my *desiring* to have one!

Here a misunderstanding is likely to arise. I once told a close friend of mine (who incidentally believed in God but thoroughly disbelieved in an afterlife) that I could form no idea whatsoever of my own nonexistence. He replied, "Oh, come on now; of course you can!"

I replied, "How can *you* know what *I* am or am not capable of imagining? If you wish to claim that *you* are incapable of imagining *your* nonexistence, that's a different story, but then I'd like to ask you just how you imagine it."

I got the rather standard reply: "A dreamless sleep."

Ah, a dreamless sleep! Let me talk about that for a moment. Sometimes when I ask someone what he imagines when he thinks of his nonexistence, I get the reply "a *deep* sleep." Let me talk about that first. Of course, I can imagine myself in a permanent state of deep sleep, since I have experienced deep sleep and know what it is like. But if *that's* what happens to me after my death—that I am in a deep sleep for all eternity—I would certainly regard that as a form of afterlife! By *no* afterlife I mean total annihilation—simple cessation of existence. And how can being in a deep sleep be the same as not existing at all? When I say that I believe that I will have an afterlife, I don't mean that I'll necessarily be *awake* in it; I have no idea what proportion of the time I would be awake or asleep. But at any rate, I believe that one can't be in a deep sleep without existing at the time; hence I regard a deep sleep as one possible form of an afterlife. Now, a *dreamless* sleep may be a different story, depending on what is meant by the term. Does it mean a state where one has absolutely no consciousness whatsoever, where one has *no* experiences at all? Such a state would indeed qualify as no afterlife, but then I don't believe one can imagine oneself in such a state! In the first place, it is extremely doubtful that, at any stage of our lives, we are ever in a state in which we have *no* experiences whatsoever (there is surely always *some* brain activity going on), so I don't believe we have ever been in a completely consciousless sleep. More importantly, even if we have, we couldn't possibly *experience* it (it is logically impossible to experience a state in which we have no experiences at all); hence, I don't see how we can remember being in such a state (how can we remember anything other than a past experience?); hence I don't see how we can *imagine* such a state. And so in short, if a dreamless sleep means a completely consciousless state, I don't believe we can imagine being in it. On the other hand, if a dreamless sleep involves *some* rudiment of consciousness, then being in a dreamless sleep after death is conceivable, but would then constitute a kind of afterlife. And so, I believe that my inability to conceive of no afterlife is a far more potent factor in my belief in an afterlife than any *desire* for an afterlife (though my desire is certainly present.)

It is here that my attitude differs from that of Gardner and Unamuno. They claim that they believe in God and an afterlife because their hearts desire these things. Leaving God aside for the moment, I suspect that the *real* reason they believe in an afterlife is their inability to conceive of any other possibility. Thus, I think the Freudian explanation comes closer to the truth than the hypothesis of wishful thinking. Actually, Unamuno says elsewhere in his book *The Tragic Sense of Life* much the same thing that I am saying. He says:

> It is impossible for us, in effect, to conceive of ourselves as not existing, and no effort is capable of enabling consciousness to realize absolute unconsciousness, its own annihilation. Try, reader, to imagine yourself, when you are wide awake, the condition of your soul when you are in a deep sleep; try to fill your consciousness with the representation of no-consciousness, and you will see the impossibility of it. The effort to comprehend it causes the most tormenting dizziness. We cannot conceive of ourselves as not existing. (Unamuno 1889, p. 38)

I agree with him, of course (except that I would substitute "consciousless sleep" for "deep sleep"), but I find it puzzling that elsewhere in the book (in fact, many times) Unamuno describes his utter horror at the thought of his own nonexistence. What I can't figure out is how one can be horrified at something he *can't even imagine!* He says that he can't imagine his own nonexistence, and then says that he is horrified by it! He must certainly have had *some* idea of what it was that was horrifying him.

Not everybody agrees with the statement that we cannot imagine our own nonexistence. Some people have claimed that they can. One person with whom I was discussing this—a materialistic atheist who believes that there is no possibility at all of an afterlife—said to me, "Instead of trying to imagine one's own nonexistence, what about thinking of the rest of the world?" Of all the attitudes a nonbeliever in the afterlife can take, this really strikes me as the most sensible. But even here, as Freud says, we somehow imagine ourselves as spectators. There is another thing I would like to point out: I know some atheists who deny the existence of the soul, who deny an afterlife, and who think of death as a dreamless sleep. Some of them (whom I have asked) even believe that before they were born, they were in a state of dreamless sleep. This seems to me close to an inconsistency. *What,* if not the soul, was in a dreamless sleep? Certainly not the body, which didn't exist yet! And after life is over and the body has long since become dry dust, could it be the *body* that is in a state of dreamless sleep?

Concerning the subject of God—that's a rather big subject, don't you think? Freud's belief that we all unconsciously believe in an afterlife reminds me of Calvin's belief that we all, deep down, believe in God—only Calvin goes further and claims that deep down we all *know* that there is a God. I tend to believe that Calvin is right in that we all unconsciously believe in a God, only I do not share Calvin's belief that this constitutes evidence that there *is* a God. I also believe (as does Carl Jung) that our unconscious belief in a God, coupled with our conscious rejection of the idea, is responsible for an enormous number of our neurotic disorders. Yes, I am closer to Jung than to Freud in one important respect: I believe that our unresolved *religious* conflicts play just as much a role (if not a greater one) in our neurotic problems as do our sexual conflicts, and I do not believe that the former is simply a sublimation of the latter. As I see it, we all have a kind of primal intuition of something like a God, but many of us pride ourselves on our objectivity, rationality, intelligence, freedom from primitive superstitions, scientific attitudes, etc., and so we simply *repress* this intuition to the point that we are totally unaware of it on any conscious level (and might even get upset if anyone suggests we have it!). But the intuition doesn't disappear; it simply works underground. And we wonder why we are so unhappy!

Now, please, don't get me wrong; I am *not* using this (as some people unfortunately do) as an argument for the existence of God. I frankly don't know whether there is a God or not, though I strongly believe that the belief that there is, though not wholly accurate, somehow comes closer to the truth than the belief that there isn't. I guess I should be classified as an agnostic with a leaning toward some kind of theism. However, I am not consistent even here; my attitudes toward religion vary considerably from time to time. Some people regard me as more religious than I believe I am. I am certainly intensely preoccupied with religion and mysticism, but is that the same thing as being religious? Do I have more religious consciousness than normal, or is it that I am simply more *aware* of my religious and mystical attitudes than most people are of theirs? Some people have asked me if I am a mystic. On a humorous level I would reply, "If so, I'm certainly not a very successful one!" On a more serious level, I would say that for me to call myself a mystic would be like a music lover calling himself a musician! To call myself a mystic would be far too flattering. I love mystics, I admire them, I believe they are really on to something of supreme importance, but unfortunately, I am not nearly on their level. (I wish to God I were!) However, whatever little mystic insight I have (and I believe everyone has *some*) makes me highly respectful of certain forms of pantheism. And so we are back to pantheism and Martin Gardner.

It seems that Gardner's attitude toward pantheism is largely negative, whereas mine is largely positive. He does, however, distinguish between its various forms. At the lowest level (and there I tend to agree) is the one who simply *defines* God as the totality of all there is. Now this, according to Gardner, is sheer verbal jugglery, and believing in God in this sense is tantamount to atheism. (Obviously, everybody believes in God in *that* nonstandard sense; none of us doubt *the existence of all that is!*) Yes, indeed, anybody who uses the word "God" in that sense is simply using it wrongly—that is, in violation of standard usage.

Gardner soon after says that it is hard to understand, but outspoken atheists sometimes like to talk as if they believe in God. He points out that John Dewey, in his book *A Common Faith*, suggests that God be redefined to stand for all those forces in nature and society that work to bring about the ethical ideals of humanity. He then quotes the following passage of Dewey: "It is this *active* relation between ideal and actual to which I would give the name 'God.' I would not insist that the name *must* be given. There are those that hold that the associations of the term with the supernatural are so numerous and close that any use of the word 'God' is sure to give rise to misconceptions and be taken as a concession to traditional ideas" (Gardner 1983, p. 178). This is the sort of thing that Gardner calls "verbal flimflam," and to a large extent I agree. He then points out that even Dewey's disciple Sydney Hook says that by taking over the word "God" as the religious humanists do, the waters of thought, feeling, and faith are muddied, the issues blurred, and the "word" itself becomes the object of interest and not what it signifies.

Again, I largely agree, though there is one other factor that should be taken into consideration that I will discuss a bit later. Meanwhile, I would like to relate a relevant incident: I knew a man, no longer alive, who called himself an atheist. (He gave me some weird argument that I could never really understand to the effect that a creator God violated the law of conservation of matter and energy!) His daughter, a devout believer in God, once told me, "My father wasn't an atheist; he believed that *Nature* was God!" Note, please, that the father didn't *define* God to be nature, unlike Dewey who proposed to define God in the unorthodox way he did. My guess is that the father had a *prior* conception of God and believed in fact that God and nature were really one and the same thing.

I also know of a student in a freshman philosophy class who wrote an essay, the point of which was that God, spirit, and personality are really one and the same thing. I don't believe that this is mere word play; I think she had an idea in mind which is not too far from the philosophy of the Vedanta, which is that in the last analysis, we and Brahma are ultimately the same. This is very different from *defining* Brahma to be us! The latter is only a silly definition and has no real content, whereas the former *asserts* something (whether true or false is another question).

Similarly, I believe that some pantheists have a prior conception of God and believe that God and the universe are in fact the same entity. I suspect that even though Dewey *defined* God to be those forces in nature and society that work to bring about the ethical ideals of humanity, what *really* went on psychologically is that Dewey had a *prior* conception of God—namely, as that which is demanding of our highest allegiance—and believed that it was the welfare of humanity that demanded this. And so from a *logical* point of view, although it has no significance to *define* God in the way Dewey suggested, his suggestion nevertheless conceals an important message, which is something like "We don't really know whether some transcendental spiritual being created and governs this universe, but whether or not this is so, our *duty* is to aid the ethical progress of humanity." This, I think, is what Dewey really meant. But I do believe that instead of proposing to define God in the way he did, it would have been better to have said something like "The allegiance to an unknown God and the concern with an unknown afterlife should be replaced by an allegiance to the progress of humanity and concern for this life." That at least would have been an unequivocal credo. Better yet, so as not to antagonize any religious sensibilities, he might have said, "Whatever you may believe about a supernatural God and an afterlife, please remember your duties to humanity and progress in this life!" No one—religious or otherwise—could have objected to that! What he calls a "common faith" is indeed common to religious and nonreligious people alike.

Now, is defining God to be the entire universe mere verbal jugglery? Logically, yes, but psychologically, I'm not so sure. The word "God" has a sort of magical, mystical, numinous, and reverential aura about it, and so it may well be that when someone defines God to be the universe, his *subconscious* purpose in doing so is to invest the universe with this aura! I suggest that by just calling the universe "God," he may well have a different emotional (even religious) attitude toward the universe than if he doesn't. And so perhaps what Gardner calls mere verbal jugglery has a deeper psychological significance than meets the eye.

At any rate, this is *not* the kind of pantheism in which I am really interested. I am far more interested in that form of pantheism (sometimes called *panpsychism*, or as Charles Hartshorne has suggested, *panentheism*) which views God as a World Soul, a consciousness that arises from the structure of the universe in a way similar to the way our consciousness arises out of our bodily structures. In other words, just as a mind is attached to each of our bodies, a great cosmic mind is attached to the universe as a whole—the universe thinks! Personally, I find this an extremely attractive and inspiring idea—far more so than any of the organized religions. I also tend to think of the World Soul (as did Samuel Alexander) as evolving and *approaching* final perfection, but maybe never reaching it.

Gardner quotes a marvelous passage in Percy Bysshe Shelley's essay "The Necessity of Atheism" and compliments Shelley for his honesty in calling himself an atheist. Shelley's essay begins "There is no God." But he immediately adds, "This negation must be understood solely to effect a creative deity. The hypothesis of a pervading spirit co-eternal with the universe remains unshaken."

I love that phrase "pervading spirit co-eternal with the universe," and to call this "atheism" is utterly crazy! A spirit co-eternal with the universe! What better God could one want? To me, this is far more important than a mere verbal dispute; I want to reserve the word "God" to mean that which is highest and best, and to me, Shelley's *pervading spirit co-eternal with the universe* fits the bill far better than the God of any of the world's organized religions—or even the personal God of the theists!

Now, let me cool down and continue with Martin Gardner's book. His chapter 12 is entitled "The Proofs: Why I Do Not Believe God's Existence Can Be Demonstrated." I have little to say about this chapter, since I largely agree. The ontological arguments (arguments from pure reason) are so obviously flawed that I am amazed that any intelligent minds could have thought them up (and philosophers like Descartes certainly were intelligent!). The cosmological argument, it seems to me, fares somewhat better, and, although not amounting to a *proof,* has some appeal to the reason of at least some of us. (Assuming the big bang theory to be true, isn't it more difficult to believe that the universe came out of nothing *all by itself* than that there was some mind present to supervise the process?) As for the argument from design, I have already said that it does not constitute a proof, but has *some* appeal to reason. And so, in short, I agree that God's existence cannot be demonstrated, but I don't see the cosmological and design arguments as completely valueless (as are the ontological arguments). They are suggestive and have *some* appeal to our reason (or at least the reason of some of us).

Gardner's next chapter is entitled "Faith: Why I Am Not an Atheist." William James tells of the incident in which he asked a schoolboy whether he knew what faith is. The boy answered, "Yeah, faith is when you believe something you know ain't true."

Gardner quotes Bertrand Russell as having once defined faith as "a firm belief in something for which there is no evidence." Gardner says that Russell's definition seems to him to be concise and admirable. I myself have two criticisms of the definition. First, it would be better to say, "a firm belief in something for which the *believer* has no evidence." My point, of course, is that even if there is evidence for a belief, if the believer does not know of the evidence, his belief is based purely on faith. Actually, even this is not adequate, which brings me to my second and more important criticism: I say that faith must involve some element of hope, some desire that the proposition in question be true. One can hardly have faith in something one hopes is false! For example, if a sick person believes without evidence that he will get worse, it is most unlikely that he would say, "I have faith that I will get worse." On the other hand, if he believes without evidence that he will get better, then he could very well say, "I have faith that I will get better." Or again, people have said that they have faith in the existence of God, but has anyone ever said that he has *faith* in the existence of the devil? Of course, a person might say that his faith requires him to believe in the devil, but this is something very different.

Actually, even hope is not enough; a person might, for example, hope that his enemy will die, but it is unlikely that he would say, "I have faith that he will die." In addition to hope, there must also be the belief that the thing hoped for must be *good*. In fact, I'd say that the belief in the goodness of the thing hoped for may be even more basic than the hope. And so, I propose that Russell's definition of faith be emended to read "Belief not based on evidence in something hoped for and believed to be good."

There is, however, another aspect of faith that the above emendation does not capture: I once thought of defining faith as the preference for believing something, and being wrong, to disbelieving it and being right. For example, if one would rather believe in an afterlife and be wrong than believe there is no afterlife and be right, I would say that he has faith in an afterlife. (I think Unamuno might have liked that definition.) Actually, Unamuno thinks of faith as just that which others call "wishful thinking." He candidly says:

Faith is in its essence simply a matter of will, not of reason, that to believe is to wish to believe, and to believe in God is, before all and above all, to wish that there may be a God. In the same way, to believe in the immortality of the soul, is to wish that the soul may be immortal, but to wish it with such force that this volition shall trample reason under foot and pass beyond it. But reason has its revenge. (Unamuno 1889, p. 114)

I disagree with Unamuno that faith must go *against* reason! True, faith may be *unsupported* by reason, but that does not mean that it is necessarily *opposed* to reason. Yet Unamuno believes in the opposition and seems to relish it! I think that if he had found reasons to support his faith, he would actually have been disappointed! He seems to have had a deep psychological need of the tension that he believes to exist between the two.

Concerning beliefs that are held without evidence, I wonder what percentage of them are true. Does anyone know? Could any statistical research on this shed any light? Suppose it could, and it turned out that of all the beliefs based purely on faith, an overwhelming proportion of them turned out to be true. Then, for the first time, it would be *rationally* justified to trust our beliefs based on faith. I wonder how Unamuno would react if he had known about this. How would he have reacted if people had told him, "You are very wise to trust your faith! It has been scientifically established that beliefs based on faith are far more likely to be true than false. You are really doing a very rational thing!" (I bet Unamuno would have been furious!)

I have also been intrigued by a related problem: If one has a conflict between one's reason and intuition, which should one trust? Some people tell me that one should trust one's reason, but how do they know? Others say that one should trust one's intuition, but how do *they* know? Does anyone know? Could any objective research settle this?

Concerning people's denial of their need for an afterlife, Unamuno has this to say:

Those who say that they have no need of any faith in an eternal personal life to furnish them with incentives to living and motives for action, I know not well how to think. A man blind from birth may also assure us that he feels no great longing to enjoy the world of sight nor suffers any great anguish from not having enjoyed it, and we must needs believe him, for what is wholly unknown cannot be the object

> of desire . . . , there can be no volition save of things already known. But I cannot be persuaded that he who has once in his life, either in his youth or for some other brief space of time, cherished the belief in the immortality of the soul, will ever find peace without it. (p. 101)

In a similar key, Martin Gardner says:

> For many people, perhaps most people, there is a deep ineradicable desire not to cease to exist. . . . I share with Unamuno a vast incredibility when I meet individuals seemingly well adjusted and happy, who solemnly assure me they have absolutely no desire to live again. Do they really mean it? Or are they wearing a mask which they suppose fashionable while deep inside their hearts, in the middle of the night and in moments of agony, they secretly hope to be surprised one day by the existence and mercy of God? (Gardner 1983, p. 213)

Again, Gardner ties up belief in immortality with belief in God! I wish he had rather ended the question with something like "they secretly hope to be surprised one day by finding out that there is an afterlife after all." And this brings me to the recollection of the following relevant and delightful incident.

I was having dinner with a married couple—two very close friends—both of whom are staunch materialists and atheists and who definitely disbelieve in any afterlife. The wife said, "The fact that our lives are only of finite duration is precisely what gives them their value; we can only appreciate things that are rare. If my life were endless, it would be commonplace, hence it would lose its value." She asked me if I agreed, and when I told her that I certainly did not, she said that she was surprised. I then asked her husband whether he agreed, and he said *yes*. I then said, "You mean to say that if to your surprise you found yourself alive again after you died, you would be *disappointed?*" He laughed heartily and said, "Of course not! I would be delighted! I think it would be beautiful if there were a God and an afterlife." (Interestingly enough, he also brought God into the picture!) I was amused at his obvious inconsistency, but delighted with his honesty. I asked the wife whether she would be disappointed. She replied, "I find the idea of an afterlife so inconceivable that I cannot say." Incidentally, she is a biologist, which might in part explain her inability to even *conceive* of the idea of an afterlife. She once told me that she regarded the afterlife as not only improbable, but as impossible! The husband, on the other hand, believes an afterlife to be highly improbable, but not impossible. (His view here is the same as that of Bertrand Russell.) He also once said to a group of us, "I think it would be beautiful if there were a God!" Someone present asked, "Then why don't you believe in one?" He replied, "Because I think the idea is ridiculous!"

On another occasion, the wife asked me if I believed in God. I replied that I had absolutely no way of knowing. She then said that she felt that the question was so important that one *should* make up one's mind one way or another. (She, of course, had opted for atheism.) I told her that I thought that was ridiculous! If a person wants to make up his mind one way or another, there is certainly no reason that he shouldn't, but that's no reason why he *should*, if he doesn't want to! What's wrong with a person who wishes to take a purely objective, scientific attitude and say that he reserves judgment because he doesn't have enough evidence?

On another occasion, she told me that she was afraid that if she should ever believe in God, then she would join some organized religion. I found that most revealing! I was particularly interested in light of the fact that I had read somewhere in a book by Nicholas Berdyaev (I'm not sure which, but I think it was *Dream and Reality*) that from his observations, when materialistic atheists turn to believing in God, they usually convert to an orthodox religion. Whereas idealistic atheists, if they later believe in God, do not.

I once had the following brief religious conversation with a friend, which strikes me as rather funny. I asked him, "Do you believe in God?"

He replied, "I certainly believe in something!"

I replied that I also believe in something, but don't know what that something is!

He replied, "That's how I feel."

End of conversation!

Gardner says that he agrees with Bayle and with Unamuno that when cold reason contemplates the world, it finds not only an absence of God, but good reasons for supposing there is no God at all. A bit later he says, "To a rational mind the world *looks* like a world without God. It *looks* like a world with no hope for another life" (p. 214).

How strange! As I have indicated before, in *one* way the world looks as if there is no God (because of the existence of evil, for one thing), and in *another* way the world looks as if there is a God (because of its fantastic design). But I am even more puzzled by Gardner's second sentence: How would a world in which the inhabitants do have an afterlife *look* any different from one in which the inhabitants don't? How can one tell by *looking* at the world whether its inhabitants have an afterlife? I am reminded of a delightful Haiku:

> There is nothing in the voice of the cicada
> To indicate
> How long it will live.

Many people have claimed that the weight of scientific evidence is all *against* survival (and Unamuno and Gardner agree). I believe that this question is an extremely important one, and I am doubtful that it has been adequately treated by philosophers of science. I wish now to consider the question from a purely scientific perspective and leave out religious considerations altogether.

My thesis is that there isn't the slightest bit of scientific evidence for or against survival. Now, a standard argument against the possibility of survival is that there is no positive evidence for it (spiritualism and psychic research have been discredited), and the lack of such positive evidence constitutes some degree of negative evidence. This, by the way, is Gardner's view as revealed in a private communication. Now, I certainly agree with the first part—there is no evidence for survival—but I disagree with the second. Someone once asked me, "Don't you believe that the fact that sightings of flying saucers have been discredited constitutes evidence that there are no flying saucers?" Well, now, the analogy is not a good one. Flying saucers are physical objects that can be directly observed by purely scientific means; spirits are not. All science can observe of spirits are their possible physical manifestations—and these can be explained by purely naturalistic means. Also, with respect to flying saucers, from the fact that there has been no reliable evidence of their detection here, I grant that it certainly *does* follow that the odds are strongly against there ever having been any flying saucers visiting our planet, but it certainly does *not* constitute evidence against the existence of flying saucers! (Indeed, it is perfectly reasonable that there may be alien spaceships elsewhere in the universe.) Similarly, the fact that there is no reliable evidence that the living have ever communicated with departed spirits constitutes strong probabilistic evidence that the living have never yet established such communication and, most likely, never will. But is it scientifically legitimate to conclude that there *are* no departed souls?

The point is that there is such a thing as well-designed and poorly designed experiments—in brief, *good* and *bad* experiments. Well, the experiments of mediums strike me as incredibly bad! Why on earth should one expect that because a medium goes into a trance, a departed spirit should take over his or her body? For that matter, suppose I light a fire in my fireplace, hoping that in the middle of the night, after the fire goes out, a departed spirit will write a message in the ashes. The next morning, there is no message. Suppose this experiment is repeated millions of times and always with negative results. What conclusion should be drawn? That there are probably no departed spirits? No. The right conclusion is that if there are any spirits, they don't write messages in ashes.

My whole point, of course, is that spiritualism and survival are very different things, and that the negative results of spiritualistic investigation do confirm that spiritualism is probably false, but casts no light on the probability of survival.

Let me put my case more strongly. Consider the following hypothesis: *There is an afterlife, but departed spirits are on a plane totally separated from this one, and no communication with them is possible.* I am not asserting that this hypothesis is true, but only that, true or false, *it is totally immune to scientific investigation!* (Indeed, many logical positivists would declare the hypothesis to be neither true nor false, but meaningless, since there is in principle no way of either verifying or refuting it.)

Let us consider a related point. Suppose a person inclined toward materialism is skeptical about the existence of souls altogether. Is there any scientific experiment one could perform to test whether there are souls? I know of only one experiment that has been tried (and I call this a good experiment)—namely, weighing a person just before and just after he dies. Of course, there was no loss in weight. Is a materialist, therefore, justified in concluding that there are probably no souls? Of course not; the correct conclusion is that, if souls exist, they have no weight. (I can't help but recall a delightful saying of Confucius about spirits: "Respect spirits, if there are any, but keep aloof from them!") Incidentally, has anyone ever performed any scientific experiment to test whether God exists? The thought strikes me as quite funny!

To consider my point in its full generality, suppose we define the *nonmaterial* as that which (if it exists) is not observable by any physical scientific means whatsoever. Now, how could physical science possibly design any experiment to determine the existence of the nonmaterial? The fact that it can't is hardly more than a tautology!

Now, a word as to why I believe this whole issue is of *psychological* importance. Not everybody is like Unamuno in that he is willing to make a leap of faith into something for which there is evidence *against*. There are many (like myself) who have no problem at all in believing things for which there is no evidence one way or the other, but who feel uneasy at believing things *contrary* to scientific evidence. I believe that many people *intuitively* believe or feel that there is an afterlife, but repress their feelings because they regard them as "unscientific." I wish to urge that the belief in an afterlife is neither unscientific nor scientific, but completely tangential to science. I think it would be helpful if this were generally recognized.

I suspect that people like Unamuno take *extra* delight in feeling that their beliefs go *against* reason, rather than merely unsupported by reason, since it makes their "leap of faith" more defiant and heroic. The extreme of this, of course, is Tertullian who said, "I believe *because* it is absurd!" Isn't there a slight air of bravado in this? Couldn't he have been satisfied with the more modest statement "I believe, although I cannot prove it"? (I must admit, though, that I do find something intriguing and delightful in Tertullian's more drastic statement!)

Coming back to the question of whether there is any evidence for or against an afterlife, I recall that as a child, when people would tell me that there is an afterlife, I would think, "How in the world could they know?" And when, later as an adult, people would tell me that there is no afterlife—that the belief in one was only childish, egocentric, primitive, superstitious wishful thinking—I would think, "How in the world could *they* possibly know?"

I am saddened by one thing: All right, if a person believes there is no afterlife and also honestly has no desire for one, then there is nothing more to be said. But if a person *wants* an afterlife and is unhappy because he believes there isn't one (or at least probably isn't) one, I can only ask, Why give up so easily?

There is one attitude of Unamuno that I definitely do *not* share —namely, his contempt for people who do not believe in an afterlife (and especially people who claim that they don't even want one—such people he calls "monsters"). But I have often been intrigued and puzzled by why it is that some people get so irritated —so *angry*—at the mention that there *might* be an afterlife! I recall that I was once speaking to a friend—an eminent physical chemist —and I took the point of view that physical science couldn't *in principle* provide the slightest evidence for or against an afterlife. In the middle of my argument, to my great surprise, he interrupted me and said in a most angry and passionate tone, "*I don't believe it!*"

I replied, "You don't believe what—that there is an afterlife?"

He replied, "Yes."

I then tried to explain that I was not arguing that there *is* an afterlife, but only that science has nothing to say one way or the other about it.

Now, he is a very intelligent man; why did he misunderstand the point of my argument, and why was he so emotionally upset? I have known others to get equally upset and angrily declare, "I don't believe in an afterlife!"

In *The Tragic Sense of Life*, Unamuno, speaking of the Acts of the Apostles in his chapter "The Hunger for Immortality," has this to say:

> Here Paul stands before the subtle Athenians—and speaks to them as it was fitting to speak to the cultured citizens of Athens, and all listened to him, agog to hear the latest novelty. But when he speaks to them of the resurrection of the dead, their stock of patience and tolerance comes to an end, and some mock him and others say: "We will hear thee again of this matter!" intending not to hear him. . . . And in his audience before King Agrippa, when Festus the governor heard him speak of the resurrection of the dead, he exclaimed: "Thou art mad, Paul; much learning hath made thee mad." (Acts 26:24)

Unamuno then continues:

> Whatever of truth there may have been in Paul's discourse in the Areopagus, and even if there were none, it is certain that this admirable account plainly shows how far Attic tolerance goes and where the patience of the intellectuals ends. They all listen to you, calmly and smilingly, and at times they encourage you, saying: "That's strange!" or, "He has brains!" or "That's suggestive," or "How fine!" or "Pity that a thing so beautiful should not be true!" or "This makes one think!"

> But as soon as you speak to them of resurrection and life after death, they lose patience and cut short your remarks and exclaim, "Enough of this! We will talk of this another day!" (Unamuno 1889, p. 49)

Thus Unamuno clearly realized how much anxiety and hostility some people evince toward the idea of an afterlife. What is the cause? Here Unamuno has an interesting idea: "And even if this belief be absurd, why is its exposition less tolerated than that of others much more absurd? Why this manifest hostility to such a belief? Is it fear? Is it, perhaps, spite provoked by inability to share it?" (p. 50).

I must say that this last idea struck me forcibly—it is one that never occurred to me before. Could it really be spite provoked by inability to share the belief? I wouldn't be surprised if this is so in *some* cases, but I can think of another explanation—fear of having false hopes! To begin with, why are some people so dogged in their belief that there *definitely* is no afterlife? They give so-called "rational scientific" arguments, which, in fact, are extremely poor (for reasons I have indicated), and which are nothing more than sheer rationalizations. Then what is the real cause of the insistence? I believe that it is often that they don't want to believe in or even hope for something which may never come about; they are frightened of the thought of living in a fool's paradise. And so they would *love* to have an afterlife but believe that it is wrong to hope for one—it is *ignoble* to indulge in this egocentric kind of wishful thinking. And so when someone suggests to them that there might be an afterlife after all, their anxieties are aroused by their struggle to resist *the temptation of indulging in wishful thinking!* If I am right, then perhaps it is cruel to suggest to a person who doesn't believe in an afterlife that maybe there is one! Maybe I am being cruel to some of my readers by writing all this! If so, I apologize.

In his next chapter, "The Rationalist Dissolution," Unamuno says, "The anti-theological hate, the scientificist—I do not say scientific—fury, is manifest. Consider, not the more detached scientific investigators, those who know how to doubt, but the fanatics of rationalism, and observe with what gross brutality they speak of faith" (p. 95). I was delighted with Unamuno's phrase "the fanatics of rationalism." They are certainly of a very different breed from those who are rational! It has been my lifelong experience that those who most "wave the flag of rationality" are those with the most irrational prejudices! The most rational people I know have the good sense to know when rationality is appropriate and when it isn't. A bit later, Unamuno says, "There are people who seem not to be content with not believing that there is another life, or rather with believing that there is none, but who are vexed and hurt that others should believe in it or should even wish that it might exist" (pp. 95–96).

Actually, Unamuno, I'm afraid, does somewhat the same in the reverse direction! He seems to somehow look down on those who don't share his belief in God and an afterlife. His attitude toward them is often condemning. It's almost as if he's afraid that those who disbelieve in an afterlife somehow have the power to prevent us from having one! (Maybe deep down he regards the matter as a *voting* issue—if enough people vote for an afterlife, then there will be one!)

I must tell you of something very funny that I read some time ago in some book or other on the philosophy of religion. It's the sort of thing that could be told as a joke but was actually true. It's about a Catholic priest, a Protestant minister, and a rabbi (aren't there many jokes that begin like this?) being interviewed and relating their experiences in trying to console dying patients. The minister said that most of the patients he encountered had more faith than he did—they looked forward to a blissful life in heaven, and the minister, though less sure, felt that this was not the time to argue. The priest said that he believed that he had provided definite consolation to the patients. As to the rabbi, he said, "All one can do for a dying Jew is to get him better!"

Returning to Gardner's book, he next says a little about mysticism: "Persons of strong faith sometimes say they have a direct awareness of God, a knowledge of the sort that philosophers have called knowledge by acquaintance. Mystics claim to have perceived God in a manner analogous to looking at the sun. We shall not linger over these claims. They carry no weight with anyone who has not had such an experience" (Gardner 1983, p. 214). That last statement can't be true! There are surely many people who have never had any mystical experiences themselves, but nevertheless trust the mystical testimonies of others. Wasn't William James one such person? I myself certainly do take the mystical experiences of others quite seriously, even though it is questionable whether I have ever had any experience that would qualify as "mystical." I certainly agree with Gardner when he next says that no empirical tests can confirm that a person who professes such contact with God is actually in such contact and that in many cases of persons who claimed such visions, there is good evidence that they were experiencing delusions. Of course, no empirical test can confirm the mystical insights of another person, but some of us have *faith* in mysticism—just as Gardner has faith in God and an afterlife.

Mohammed made one marvelous comment about people who believe in God but who have never experienced God. He said, "It's like a donkey carrying a load of books." (Of all the things that I know of that Mohammed said, I like this best!) I was also delighted with the following bit I came across in the book *River of Light* by Rabbi Laurence Kushner. He quotes a Midrash (story built on a story) about Abraham and Isaac in which, after a three-day journey, Abraham looked up and saw the cloud of God's presence on the mountain. Turning to Isaac, he said, "Do you see it too, my son?"

"Yes, my father, I see it too."

Then he turned to the two servants. "Do you see it?"

"No," they said. "We don't see anything."

Abraham replied to his servants, "You stay here with the donkey, because he doesn't see anything either!"

Now I would like to say a little about William James. I always found it so sad that he had to work so hard apologizing for beliefs based purely on faith. In later years he said about his famous essay, "The Will to Believe," that he should have called it "The Right to Believe." Well, of course, one has the right to believe; how can there be any doubt about it? Again, has anyone ever proved that beliefs based purely on faith are more likely to be false than true?

There is something that should be pointed out about "proofs" for or against the existence of God—namely, that, except in the exact sciences, the word "proof" appears to have no objective or uniform meaning. I strongly suspect that the notion is far more subjective than is generally realized and that what constitutes a "proof" to one person is simply no proof at all to another. Except in mathematics, where the notion of a proof within a given system has been precisely defined, what really is a proof except an argument that convinces somebody? And different people are convinced by different arguments. Similar remarks apply to the expression "known by reason."

As a perfect case in point, a Catholic once told me that the existence of God cannot be known by pure reason—a leap in faith is necessary—but once granted that there is a God, it can be proved by pure reason that Catholicism is the true religion. I asked her how this could be proved. She replied, "Well, if there is a God, isn't it natural that He would want to communicate with us?" I replied, "Not by such a roundabout process as inspiring people to write a Bible and then expecting others to believe that it was really written by God! If God wishes to communicate with us, why doesn't He do so directly instead of playing those hide-and-seek games?" She replied, "Ah, that has been a long-time mystery to theologians!"

Well, that's as far as we were able to get. We got stymied almost at the very start. Her sense of reason evidently told her that if there is a God, then God would want to communicate with us, hence He wrote the Bible. My sense of reason told me no such thing. And so it was painfully obvious that we meant different things by "knowable by reason."

Coming back to Gardner's book, after the next chapter on prayer, he devotes two chapters to the problem of evil—"Evil: Why?" and "Evil: Why We Don't Know Why." His two major points are (1) We don't know why there is evil; (2) God has His reasons for wanting us not to know why.

Much of the arguments are standard, and, as I have already said, none of these arguments are logically disprovable, yet they all seem contrived and implausible. The most reasonable explanation in my mind of the existence of evil, other than a purely atheistic one, is that of an *evolving* deity. And this brings me to my main theological difference with Martin Gardner. Gardner uses the phrase "finite God," which I find inappropriate, for what I call an *evolving* deity. He says that the word "infinite" has a different meaning when applied to God (whom he believes *is* infinite, in whatever sense he has in mind). I myself prefer to use the terms *finite* and *infinite* only in their ordinary sense, and so I shall talk of an *evolving* Deity as contrasted with a *perfect* (or *all-powerful*) God.

It is amazing the degree of prejudice that exists toward the notion of an *evolving* God! Even atheists express their contempt and say, "Now, *what* kind of God is that?" Their attitude seems to be "I don't believe in God, but if you're going to give me one, for Heaven's sake, give me a *real* God and not a mockery!" I know one lady, an ex-Catholic, now inclined toward a position about midway between atheism and agnosticism, but who often shakes her fist in anger against God for allowing the terrible evils of the world, who, when I mentioned the possibility of an *evolving* God, thought this the most ridiculous position of all.

Now, I can understand that one brought up in an orthodox religion that demands belief in an all-powerful God would find the idea of an *evolving* God unacceptable. As one Catholic once said to me, "That's not much of a God, is it?" Well, to me, an evolving God *is* much of a God, and the existence of such a God strikes me as far more plausible than either the idea that there is a perfect God or that there is no God at all.

In the last analysis, I doubt that any of these three models exactly capture the truth, but I believe that the model of an evolving deity comes the closest. This is what is sometimes known as *process* theology and is the philosophy of thinkers like Samuel Alexander, Alfred North Whitehead, and (of more recent times) Charles Hartshorne. In this intriguing model, God is getting progressively better and better, and in our struggle against evil, we are actually *assisting* God in his own development!

Incidentally, Gardner's attitude toward Hartshorne strikes me as quite amusing; I wouldn't be surprised if the two had some lively arguments together! Speaking of the vision of a finite God, Gardner says:

> No one has defended this vision with more skill than Charles Hartshorne, one of my fondly recalled teachers at the University of Chicago. Only this model, he passionately believes, will solve the problem of evil for a theist. Hartshorne's writings are stimulating to read and seldom opaque, but I am always made uncomfortable by the fact that he seems to know more about God than I do. (Gardner 1983, p. 251)

I must digress with an amusing memory of Charles Hartshorne. I was visiting the University of Texas, where Hartshorne was then teaching, and I got into a lively philosophical discussion with him and the logical positivist Oswald Bowsma, who was also teaching there at the time. I was taking an ultra-idealistic position, maintaining that minds can exist without bodies and can easily change bodies from time to time.

I said, "I'm perfectly prepared for the possibility that in two weeks I'll find myself in a body with three arms."

Bowsma (in his practical way) said, "You are really prepared?"

I said, "Yes."

He said, "I mean, you've gotten yourself a third glove?"

This got a general laugh. I then turned to Hartshorne and said, "Tell me, do you believe that what I'm saying is inconsistent?"

He replied, "What you are saying is too *vague* to be inconsistent!"

Coming back to what Martin said about Hartshorne, I wonder who *does* know more about God, Gardner or Hartshorne? Now, isn't the question ridiculous? Does anyone know anything *more* than anyone else about God? Does anyone *know* anything about God? I doubt it!

Coming back to the subject of an *evolving* deity, is there any doubt from a purely *rational* point of view that the hypothesis of such a deity is more likely than that of a perfect God? Just look around you; does this really suggest a *perfect* God? But, of course, many feel that they need a perfect God. But why? Can't one pray to an evolving deity for forgiveness of one's sins (or better still, for help in stopping sinning)? And why can't an evolving deity be powerful enough to give us an afterlife?

I must again digress by telling you two delightful incidents I recently read about. The first is about Bertrand Russell, who was once speaking with his old friend Robert Trevelyan, and the conversation turned to theology. Trevelyan said, "The trouble is, I somehow don't seem to be able to get interested in God." Russell replied, "Perhaps it's mutual!"

The second incident concerns two friends in England who were talking of a mutual friend, and one said, "What do you think of his just having been appointed a judge?"

The other replied, "He could have risen higher than that; he could have risen to being a bishop!"

The first said, "What do you mean by that? In what sense is a bishop higher than a judge?"

The other replied, "All a judge can say is 'You be hanged!'; whereas a bishop can say, 'You be damned!'"

"Yes," said the first one, "but the difference is that when a judge says, 'You be hanged,' you really get hanged!"

Coming back to the problem of evil, I don't go as far as Hartshorne in believing that the evolving God hypothesis provides the *only* theologically acceptable solution, but I do believe that it provides the best one.

There is another model well worth considering—that provided by the Indian philosophy of the Vedanta. According to this, there is the higher Brahma and the lower Brahma. The lower Brahma is a personal deity to whom we can pray—much like the God of the Old Testament. The higher Brahma is a much more mysterious and abstract being (sometimes identified as pure existence, pure consciousness, pure bliss) that has no predicates at all and is somewhat like the God of Maimonides (who was regarded as heretical by many of his theological contemporaries). The Vedantic philosophers believe, however, that the average person cannot comprehend the higher Brahma, and hence must worship the lower one.

I like this model very much and am far more interested in the higher Brahma than the lower. (I think that if I followed the Hindu faith, I would try to circumvent the lower Brahma altogether and directly approach the higher one.) This Indian model comes close to the Cosmic Consciousness model of Richard Bucke and Edward Carpenter, which is my favorite model of all and of which I will say more in my third part of this book.

I fortunately own a marvelous book, *Indian Thought, Past and Present,* by R. W. Frazer, which contains the following passages:

> India for the past thirty centuries has brooded over the problem of the Universe. She has ceaselessly striven for some satisfactory answers to the question of the How and Whence and Wherefore of it all. . . .
>
> In one of the earliest sacred books [the Vedas] is said: Who knows and who can tell how all arose or whence it came? The gods know not, for they came later. He in the highest heaven knows the source whence came all things. He knows if there was creation or non-creation, or perchance He knows not. (Frazer 1915, pp. 7, 16)

(I hope the reader appreciates that last bit of modesty and lack of dogmatism!)

It seems to me that it might be possible to combine the Brahmanic model of the two Brahmas with that of an evolving deity— namely, the higher Brahma is a perfect being existing not as an actuality, but as a Platonic ideal, and the lower Brahma is the evolving deity, existing actively and ever-moving in the direction of the higher Brahma. (Have I just invented a new religion?)

Coming back to the problem of evil, I once told the Jehovah's Witness of whom I spoke earlier that I find it most implausible that a perfect God would create an imperfect world. Now, I know the

Leibnizian explanation that, although this world is imperfect, it is nevertheless the best of all possible worlds, hence is the one that God actualized. But to my amazement, the Jehovah's Witness claimed that the world *is* perfect!

"Oh come on now," I replied. "With all the evil and suffering that goes on?"

He replied, "Now, what would you have had God do—create a race of happy, well-behaved robots?"

I find this comparison so inept! For one thing, robots do *not* have consciousness. Second, there is this amazingly commonplace but pernicious error that a being must have some evil temptations to resist in order to have free will! Where did this hideous idea ever come from? I recall that an extremely learned orthodox rabbi, who believes that God created angels, once told me that angels are in such close sight of God and His goodness that they haven't the slightest temptation to sin *and hence they have no free will!* I again ask where this idea ever came from! Does it mean that those of us who are destined to go to heaven and become angels are destined to lose our free will?

One thing I do like about the Jehovah's Witnesses is that they don't believe in everlasting punishment. They (like orthodox Jews and Seventh-Day Adventists) believe in the ultimate annihilation of the wicked. What troubles me more about this group is their belief in creationism versus evolution. Now, I don't mind if an individual prefers to believe in creationism rather than evolution—that's his business. But I do object when the person claims to have *scientific* grounds for the belief. Speaking more generally, if a person wishes to take the attitude that if science ever comes into conflict with Scriptures, he will trust Scriptures, then although I do not agree, I will not fault him for it, because he is at least being honest. But I *do* fault him if he cooks up bogus *scientific* arguments to bolster his position, for then I feel he is being fraudulent. Stated otherwise, let a person say whatever he wants *in the name of Scriptures,* but let not a person utter scientific untruths *in the name of science.*

I must tell you something very funny. Some time ago, I gave a mathematics lecture at a Midwestern university. In the evening I had dinner with the faculty at a restaurant. I pointed to one of the professors I didn't know and said, "Do you realize that you look the living image of Charles Darwin?" (He sure did!) Everyone laughed heartily. Later, I found out why the laughter was so hearty:

As one of the others told me, "He happens to be the most active creationist on the campus!"

But back to Gardner, whose next three chapters are all on immortality. For the most part, I agree with his views here, so rather than make critical comments, I will express my own thoughts. I have already indicated that I believe in some kind of an afterlife—what kind I do not know. It could be an eternal sleep (which strikes me as somehow unlikely); it could be the Catholic idea of bodily resurrection (which strikes me as *extremely* unlikely!). No, the two possibilities that strike me as most plausible are either existence in a purely spiritual realm or reincarnation. Which of the two is the more likely, I have no idea. I have no illusions of anything like a "sweet heaven," and I have hopes that there is nothing like a permanent hell. I tend to think of the next life as much like this one.

I wish to say something more about faith. Although I don't have the slightest bit of objective evidence for or against the existence of an afterlife, and although I prefer that there be one, I do *not* believe that my belief in an afterlife is based on *faith*. I already told you that I cannot conceive of *not* having an afterlife and that that is a more potent factor in my belief than any desire on my part. But even this may not fully explain my belief: there may be other factors (like Cosmic Consciousness) involved—or others of which we know nothing! So, in the last analysis, I wouldn't be surprised if the true cause of the believer's belief in an afterlife is something utterly unknown! But in my case, I refuse to credit it to faith. By contrast, let me tell you that I *do* hold an article of faith—namely, I am a Universalist and believe that we not only have afterlives, but that all of us are slowly but surely moving toward a state of perfection. Now, for this, not only do I have no evidence, but (unlike the case of an afterlife) I have no difficulty imagining that I am wrong—no difficulty in imagining that we are *not* all moving toward a state of perfection. And so I, frankly, can't think of any reason for my Universalist belief other than *wishful thinking!* And so I happily plead guilty to the charge of "faith" in my Universalism. but I refuse to plead guilty to that charge when it comes to my belief in an afterlife. I make a sharp separation of the two cases.

Of course, I used the phrase "plead guilty" with tongue in cheek: Is faith—or wishful thinking, if you will—necessarily such a bad thing? Of course, it is correctly said that wishing that something is true is no guarantee that it is true. That is obvious enough. But isn't it possible that wishing might provide *some* guide to truth? Assuming for the moment that Plato was right about truth, goodness and beauty being ultimately one and the same thing, since many of our wishes are for things that are good and beautiful, might that not be some indication that they are also for something true? Of course, this is hardly a *logical* argument, but isn't it perhaps a bit suggestive? I am certainly not suggesting anything as preposterous as that *every* proposition believed as a result of wishful thinking is necessarily true (that is clearly false!), but only that wishes might constitute *some* guide to truth and should not be totally disregarded.

A few things now about reincarnation. The Zen philosopher Daisetz Suzuki has written the following excellent passage:

> I do not know whether transmigration can be proved or maintained on the scientific level, but I know that it is an inspiring theory and full of poetic suggestions, and I am satisfied with this interpretation and do not seem to have any desire to go beyond it. To me, the idea of transmigration has a personal appeal, and as to its scientific and philosophical implications, I leave it to the study of the reader. (Suzuki 1957, p. 126)

What I like is that Suzuki makes no claim that reincarnation is true or false; he just likes the idea!

I think many Americans will be surprised (and some delighted) that our dear Ben Franklin wrote the following: "Thus finding myself to exist in the world, I believe I shall, in some shape or other, always exist; and, with all the inconveniences human life is liable to, I shall not object to a new edition of mine, hoping, however, that the errata of the last may be corrected" (quoted in Head and Cranston, p. 233). One of the most sensible things I have heard said about reincarnation was said by an author named Lady Caithness in her book entitled *Old Truths in a New Light* (1876). She says, "The doctrine of metempsychosis is, above all, neither absurd nor useless. It is not more surprising to be born twice than once." My favorite passage of all on reincarnation is the following ingenious one due to the poet Heinrich Heine: "Metempsychosis often is the subject of my meditation. Who may know in what tailor now dwells the soul of Plato; in which school master the soul of a Caesar! Who knows! Possibly the soul of Pythagoras occupies the poor candidate who failed in the examination due to his inability to prove the Pythagorean theorem" (quoted ibid., p. 188).

If the reader would like to know where I stand on the question of religion, I will say briefly: I believe that just about all of the world's religions are full of myths and superstitions, but behind them all lies a vital truth. I don't believe that the religions themselves know what this truth is, but the truth is there nevertheless. By contrast, I would say that atheism, though free from the falsehoods, myths, and superstitions of the religions, has no insight into the important truths that the religions dimly but incorrectly perceive. Thus, I think of atheism as blind and the religions as having vision, but the vision is distorted. Atheism is static and is not getting anywhere; the religions, with all their faults (and the faults are many!), are at least dynamic and are slowly but surely overcoming their errors and converging to the truth. Although I attend no church, I am closer to religion as a whole than to atheism.

More specifically, my religious views come close to the idea of William James—that our unconscious is continuous and contermi-nous with a greater spiritual reality. What this reality is—whether it is personal or impersonal, conscious or unconscious, or perhaps superconscious (whatever that might mean)—is not for me to say. Actually, I go further than James in the direction of Richard Bucke's concept of Cosmic Consciousness, but I'll say more about this mag-nificent concept later in this volume.

Gardner also does not support any of the organized religions. Though brought up as a Christian, he says that in good conscience he can no longer call himself one since, for him, the doctrine of eter-nal punishment in hell is blasphemy, and he believes that there is no question that Jesus as portrayed in the Gospels believed and preached it.

Many defenders of the doctrine of eternal punishment have claimed that it has both reasonable and scriptural support. I don't doubt the latter for one second, and many regard this as the possi-ble reductio ad absurdum of Christianity. For example, Berdyaev puts it well in his book *Dream and Reality,* in which he says, "I can conceive of no more powerful and irrefutable argument in favor of atheism than the eternal torments of hell. If hell is eternal, then I am an atheist" (Berdyaev 1950, p. 293). Also, in his book *Truth and Rev-elation* he says:

> It is a highly characteristic fact that nowadays even the most orthodox creeds prefer to say much less about the eternal pains of hell. The

Roman Catholic Church, which has been fond of frightening people with hell in order to keep souls in submission, now recommends that the subject of hell not be talked about too much. If in the past the fear of hell kept people in church, nowadays it hinders them from going to church. (Berdyaev 1953, p. 128)

This was written in the early part of the last century. Is it possible that conditions have gotten worse? Surely in present-day America many Protestant evangelists and Fundamentalists are trying to scare people into conversion by threats of hell.

In a footnote, Gardner tells of Lewis Carroll, who wrote to his sister that if he were forced to believe that the God of Christians was capable of inflicting eternal punishment, he would give up Christianity. Gardner continues, "Over the centuries this has been a leading reason why many persons, including me, have given up Christianity" (Gardner 1983, p. 425).

It has been argued that the belief in hell is necessary to get people to live the good life. Here is a very insightful passage of Unamuno's in another essay:

I think that these men are mistaken who assert that they would live evilly if they did not believe in the eternal pains of hell and the mistake is all to their credit. If they ceased to believe in a sanction after death, they would not live worse, but they would look for some other ideal justification for their conduct. The good man is not good because he believes in a transcendental order, but rather he believes in it because he is good. (Unamuno 1889, p. 155)

That last sentence is marvelous! And the sentence before it shows a very interesting insight. Could it really be that some people need to find an *excuse* for being good? Also in *The Tragic Sense of Life*, Unamuno says the following: "For if a man should tell you that he does not defraud or cuckold his best friend only because he is afraid of hell, you may depend upon it that neither would he do so even if he were to cease to believe in hell, but that he would invent some other excuse instead. And this is all to the honour of the human race" (p. 262).

By contrast, let us listen to Bishop George Berkeley. In his essay "Future Rewards and Punishments" he wishes to convince freethinkers that although their *motives* may be good in trying to wean people away from the belief in eternal punishment, the effects of what they are doing are really bad. As he says,

> It is much to be feared, those well-meaning souls, while they endeav-
> oured to recommend virtue, have in reality been advancing the inter-
> ests of vice, which as I take to proceed from their ignorance of human
> nature, we may hope, when they become sensible of their mistake,
> they will, in consequence of that beneficent principle they pretend to
> act upon, reform their practice for the future. (Berkeley 1901, p. 159)

The core of Berkeley's argument is contained in the following
words:

> A man who believes in no future state would act a foolish part in
> being honest. For what reason is there why such a one should post-
> pone his own private interest or pleasure to the doing his duty? If a
> Christian foregoes some present advantage for the sake of his con-
> science, he acts accountably, because it is with the view of gaining
> some future good. But he that having no such view, should yet deny
> himself a present good in any incident where he may save appear-
> ances is altogether as stupid as he who would trust him at such a
> juncture. (p. 161)

That last sentence is really remarkable! What an ugly and *stupid*
thing to say! It's tantamount to saying that if there were no hell,
then one *shouldn't* do the right thing! There is no such thing as love
and sympathy for others or feelings of right and wrong? Fear of
hell is the *only* nonstupid reason why we should behave decently?
And Christians with their belief in hell act better on the whole than
others? This is what Berkeley seems to imply, but here he contra-
dicts something he said in an earlier essay:

> How far, I beseech you, do we Christians surpass the old heathen Ro-
> mans in temperance and fortitude, in honour and integrity? Are we
> less given to pride and avarice, strife and faction than our Pagan an-
> cestors? With us that have immortality in view, is not the old doctrine
> of "Eat and drink for tomorrow we die" as much in vogue as ever? We
> inhabitants of Christendom, enlightened with the light of the Gospel,
> instructed by the son of God, are we such shining examples of peace
> and virtue to the unconverted Gentile world? (p. 88)

So! According to this last bit, Christianity with its belief in hell
hasn't seemed to make us much better, has it? Yet, I think that in the
other essay, Berkeley does have a point worth considering: Granted that it was both ugly and stupid of Berkeley to have said that a
nonbeliever in hell would be *stupid* to act the right part (what kind

of people did Berkeley know, I wonder!), it is nevertheless true (despite Unamuno's charitable words) that *some* people are deterred from wrongdoing by the fear of hell. (Had Berkeley put it that way, I don't think anyone would have strongly objected.) As many apologists for the doctrine of everlasting punishment have said, the decline in the last century of the belief in hell is correlated with and partly the cause of the rise in crime and the lowering of moral standards. Now, although I am an extreme opponent of the doctrine of hell (for reasons I will fully discuss in Part II of this volume), I must agree that there is a good deal of truth in this claim! I really do believe that there are and have been many who would commit murder if not for their fear of hell. (They might think that they could get away with it as far as the Law is concerned, but not in God's eyes!) Still, is this an adequate justification for teaching the doctrine? I can understand the temptation to say *yes;* after all, it certainly is important to do what we can to prevent destructive acts such as murder. Still, on the whole, I must say *no,* since I believe that although the decline in the belief in hell has done some harm, it has also done much good and that *in the long run* it will be all to the good, since I cannot imagine a good world in which the belief in hell is necessary to prevent people from acting destructively.

In the last analysis, I would say that whether or not one should teach the doctrine of hell should depend entirely on whether he believes it to be *true.* If one does believe it, then of course it is his duty to teach it—not so much to prevent people from wrongdoing, but to *save* people from going there. But if one doesn't believe it, I would say it is morally wrong to teach it for the purpose of scaring one into submission. However, this is a big topic which I will discuss in Part II.

I wish now to make a few closing remarks about Gardner's book. One thing I found a bit puzzling was in the last chapter in which Gardner, speaking of the story of Jesus' raising Lazarus from the dead, says, "I can say with Spinoza, as Pierre Bayle said Spinoza said, that if I believed the truth of this legend, I would at once become a Christian" (Gardner 1983, p. 344). Does this mean that if Gardner believed the story, he would then change his mind about the reality of hell? Knowing him as I do, I can hardly believe that! But quite apart from this, what surprises me is that so many people attach so much importance to whether the miracles did or did not take place! As St. Paul said, "If Jesus be not risen, then our faith is in vain." I must ask one simple question: Why? Even if none of the miracles took place, isn't it still possible that Jesus is the incarnation of God and has the power to save souls? On the other hand, it is perfectly possible that all the miracles *did* take place and that Jesus was nevertheless no incarnation of God nor had the divine status attributed to him by orthodox Christians. Suppose I took a time machine and went back to the days of Jesus and saw with my own eyes that the miracles took place. Would that convince me of the truth of Christianity? Not one bit! And suppose *you*—my orthodox Christian reader—went back in time and saw that the miracles *didn't* take place, would that destroy your faith? If so, I think you would be very foolish! Isn't it possible that the miracles never took place and yet that Jesus was the incarnation of God?

I must say that I have less respect for those who base their faith in Christianity on the miracles than for those who base their faith on the belief that the things Jesus said are on such a high level that they must be of divine origin—no mere mortal could have said such things. (One Catholic lady I know—a psychiatrist—told me that this is the reason for her faith.) I myself do regard some of the things said by Jesus (particularly in the Fourth Gospel) to have a transcendental quality which is intensely appealing! If only he hadn't spoiled it elsewhere by his threats of hell! Perhaps the best explanation of this apparent dichotomy is that Jesus, though imperfect, was an extreme case of Cosmic Consciousness—but more of this later.

In short, I believe the important truths of Christianity to be absolutely independent of the miracles. If the miracles occurred, this does not prove the divinity of Christ (though they may constitute *some* confirming evidence). If they did not, then it is still possible that Jesus is the Way, the Truth, and the Light, and after all, isn't *that* the important thing?

Come to think of it, is it possible that anyone really *does* base his faith on the miracles? Are not the miracles rather a *bolster* for a faith that is already there? Unless one actually saw the miracles, why would he believe the report that they took place unless he had a *prior* belief in his religion? St. Paul, for example, certainly didn't believe in the New Testament miracles *before* his conversion; it was not the miracles that convinced him, but his experience on the way to Damascus of hearing the voice say, "Why persecutest thou me, Paul?" *Then* he believed in the miracles.

The whole question of the relation of miracles to faith is treated in a most beautiful and psychologically insightful manner by Martin Gardner, not in the book I have been discussing, but in his superb religious novel *The Flight of Peter Fromm* (1973). I will not spoil it by any comments of mine, other than to say that it is one of the most fascinating books I have ever read.

II *Through Dark Clouds*

A Painful Conversation

I recently had a talk with a Methodist minister, a Wesleyan. He seemed quite surprised when I told him that I have known many Christians who definitely believe in God, but do not believe in any afterlife. A disciple of his who was present said, "I'll tell you why people don't believe in an afterlife: They don't want to be accountable to God for the things they do in this life—that's why!" I replied that this may well be true in some cases, but I doubted that this was the general rule.

Incidentally, I don't in the least blame those who do not want to be accountable to God! I personally happen to have a tendency to believe in an afterlife, but I certainly resent the idea of being accountable to God! If I do a wrong act—if I injure somebody, then I want to be accountable to the *person*—or maybe to society or to the law, but certainly not to God! For that matter, if someone does me an injury, then I'd like him to settle it with *me*—or perhaps with society, or the law; I don't want God stepping in and punishing him for what the guy has done to *me*. Suppose someone did *you* an injury and the person went unpunished during his lifetime. Would you like it if God then punished him in the afterlife for what he had done to *you?*

To put the matter bluntly, I very much resent the idea of a God meddling in our affairs by punishing us for what we do to each other. Now, if God wishes to *protect* us from being harmed by others, then I would of course be most grateful. But *punishing* us in the afterlife for what we do to each other in this life hardly constitutes any protection! What would you think of a parent who stands by watching one of his children brutally mistreating another, and making not the slightest attempt to prevent it, but then *later* brutally punishing the guilty one? And isn't this just about what God does in the Jewish, Christian, and Moslem religions?

To my delight, I just came across the following passage of John Burroughs which expresses my attitude better (more calmly and less hysterically). He says: "I find I have never been burdened by a sense of my duty to God. My duty to my fellow-man and to myself is plain enough, but the word is not adequate to express any relation I may hold to the Eternal. . . . My relation to the Eternal is not that of inferior to a superior, or of a beneficiary to his benefactor, nor of a subject to his king" (Burroughs 1920, p. 50).

I wish to digress for a moment and relate a much later conversation I had with a Lutheran minister. He does believe in hell—as he put it: "After all, accounts must be settled in the next life!" At first this struck me as horrible, but after a few days of thought, I came back to him and said:

> Concerning your statement that accounts must be settled in the next life, in one sense I agree with you, and in one sense I don't. If I do someone an injury in this life and am then required in the next life to compensate him for the injury, I would regard that as perfectly fair, just, and reasonable. In *that* sense I would approve of accounts being settled in the next life. But if someone did me an injury in this life, I certainly would *not* want to see God punish him for it in the next life.

All the minister replied was "That's interesting!"

Getting back to my conversation with the Methodist minister, I then asked him the following crucial question (to me, *the* most important question in orthodox Christianity): Is God *unable* or *unwilling* to save unrepentant sinners from eternal punishment? He replied, "Unwilling. It is a matter of *justice* that unrepentant sinners suffer eternal punishment." I then said, "In other words they *deserve* eternal punishment?" To my pleasant surprise, he seemed quite reluctant to say that they *deserved* it! He would have been more consistent if he had maintained that they *did* deserve it (for how could God's punishment be just if they didn't deserve it?), but my surprise was pleasant in that I felt he was humane in doubting that they did deserve it.

He next told me (what many others have told me) that we are all born completely evil and that we can become good only by faith in Jesus Christ. I then pointed out that I have known many absolute atheists who have lived extremely good lives—even by Christian standards. Didn't *he* know any such people? He replied, "Their *actions* may be good, but this will never get them into heaven." I replied, "I never said their actions had salvation value; I merely said that they were good people."

He then said something, the shock of which has not left me to this day. It is the most utterly painful thing I have ever heard from the mouth of any Christian. He said, "Anyone who does not accept Jesus as his savior is only crucifying him a second time." Of all the unjust accusations I ever heard, this really takes the cake! Unfortunately, our conversation then came to an end, for I would have loved to ask him, "Intentionally or unintentionally?"

Postscript: I recently came across the following passage of a British writer under the pseudonym Loran Hurnscot:

> Had a rather irritable telephone conversation with my parsonical friend. I said that Buddhism was more Christian than Christianity: that in the end it promised salvation to all—it did not look on the multitude as chaff to be burned eternally. He said that there had to be a certain urgency: that with endless lives in prospect, one would always put off making the effort till the next. I said that to hinge eternal salvation on one single, confused and handicapped lifetime seemed to me a diabolical idea. He didn't agree; he said that everyone had their chance in this life, and if they wouldn't take it, "well, you've had it." If this is orthodoxy, then may God save me from it. (quoted in Head and Cranston 1968, p. 163)

Soft and Hard Christianity

I would say that the question of most *practical* importance in Christianity is whether the doctrine of eternal punishment is true or false. If true, how can the universe be anything but an infinitely hideous nightmare? How could all the joys of heaven compensate for the eternal suffering of even one soul in hell? And if the sufferer has been wicked in this life, does that make the matter any better? One can hate the actions or thoughts of an evil being, but how can one not sympathize with his suffering?

But, of course, just because those like myself see it that way—just because *we* regard the doctrine of eternal punishment as hideous—doesn't mean that the doctrine can't be true! We can *hope* that it is not; we can have *faith* that it is not—but that doesn't mean that it *is not!* Now, suppose it is true. Then comes what I regard as the most important question of all, and upon the answer depends whether those like myself can *morally* accept God or not. Is God *unable* or *unwilling* to prevent the sufferings of the damned? I would define a *soft* Christian as one who believes that God is unable, and a *hard* Christian as one who thinks God is unwilling. (If a Christian believes that there is no such thing as eternal punishment, I would call him an *ultra-soft* or *kind-hearted* Christian. Lewis Carroll is an example. Another is Nicholas Berdyaev.) Hard Christians do exist. A perfect example is St. Augustine, who said, "God could save everybody, if He wanted to. Why doesn't he? Because he will not!"

Soft Christians also exist; I have known some. One particular one is a nurse I met about forty-five years ago who tried to convert me, and my girlfriend at the time, to a fundamentalist brand of Christianity. In all honesty, I must say that she struck me as one of the most radiantly happy persons I have ever met! She never went to movies; she said, "Ever since Christ entered my heart, I have no need of such things." Her conversion (as she later reported to my girlfriend) was evidently quite sudden; after much emotional turmoil, she fell on her knees and said, "All right, God; you can have me!"

When I raised the question of *why* God allowed eternal punishment—whether He was unwilling or unable to prevent it—she took the position that He was unable—she was what I am calling a *soft* Christian. As she put it, "Salvation is a *gift*. I could stand here all night offering you a gift, but if you refuse to accept it, I cannot make you. It is the same with salvation."

I must say that her position, though ethically superior to that of a hard Christian, strikes me as quite implausible. How could an all-powerful God be *unable* to prevent the sufferings of the damned? Hard Christianity seems to me more believable than soft Christianity—though morally far more hideous!

The dilemma is clearly this: Soft Christianity seems incompatible with the omnipotence of God, and hard Christianity appears incompatible with the goodness of God. The last statement needs further elucidation by virtue of some fundamental difference in the moral sense of different individuals: Those who feel that unrepentant sinners *deserve* eternal punishment will obviously find nothing wrong with God's sanctioning this. (These are the *hard* Christians!) But those who are horrified with the idea will either be soft Christians, or (more likely) will refuse to believe that the doctrine of eternal punishment is true.

Among the hard Christians is a remarkable subgroup of people whom I would call *ultra-hard* Christians. They believe not only that eternal punishment is good and just, but that a truly good person will take positive pleasure in the sufferings of the damned! For example, Thomas Aquinas wrote, "So that the joys of the saints in heaven should be complete, they are allowed the sight of the sufferings of the damned in hell." Another obvious example of an ultra-hard Christian is Jonathan Edwards, who in his youth was horrified at the idea of eternal punishment, but who after his "conversion" found the idea "incomparably sweet."

When once I explained these painful perplexities to a Fundamentalist, he replied, "Once one has had this mystical experience, these things no longer bother one." Now, I happen to be very favorably inclined toward mysticism, but if what my friend said is true, I would regard that as a horrible black mark against mysticism! Mysticism is fine, but the last thing it should do is to make one callous!

A lot of revivalists these days seem to be ultra-hard Christians. They seem to have an awful lot of fun describing the tortures of the damned! By their behavior, they seem to be ultra-hard Christians, but I doubt that many of them quite realize this. I will save ultra-hard Christianity till later; meanwhile, I would like to say more about hard Christianity.

Is Hard Christianity Logically Consistent?

Someone once told me that he found the doctrine of eternal punishment logically inconsistent with God's goodness. I argued that the doctrine of a good God permitting eternal punishment, though morally hideous, was not *logically* inconsistent. He replied, "But our very *concept* of goodness precludes this." Well, I once took his very point of view in arguing with a Fundamentalist. I said, "My entire sense of *goodness* makes eternal punishment seem impossible." He replied (the usual answer, I believe), "*Your* concept? Who are *you*—a mere mortal—to pit your concept of goodness against that of God?"

This answer raises some fascinating basic philosophical problems! If God believes that eternal punishment is good, and I believe that it is not, is it that God *means* something different by the word "good" than I? Of course this is possible! It is certainly possible that a God who sanctions eternal punishment can be good *in His own sense of the term "good"*! But so what? Such a God appears *evil* in my sense of the term—and that is the only sense I am capable of understanding. If this should be true—if eternal punishment *is* good in God's sense—then I am neither able nor willing to love that kind of goodness. "But," someone may argue, "God's sense of goodness is *better* than yours!" To which I reply, "*Better* in my sense of the term or in His?" The obvious reply is "Better in His sense, of course!" And so the deadlock is only shifted from one word to another.

As I say, I do not believe that this point of view—the assertion that eternal punishment is good in God's sense of the word, and that my not seeing it means only that I don't have the "right" concept of goodness—this assertion seems to me logically *consistent*, but it raises one peculiar difficulty: If I can't trust my own sense of goodness, then *anything* becomes morally possible! For example, if my very sense of goodness is unreliable, then for all I know, God might punish *just* those who believe in Him and reward just those who don't. "Ridiculous!" you might say. "It goes totally against common sense!" To which I would reply, "*Whose* common sense, yours or God's?" "But," you might shout, "there is *evidence* for my position and none for yours. What *you* say goes totally against Scripture!" Ah, so it ultimately comes down to a question of evidence, does it? But surely most Christians believe that religious belief is ultimately a question of *faith*, not evidence! But in that case, how can I possibly have faith in something that strikes me as bad?

Let me now try to make a defense of hard Christianity from a different angle. Suppose that a Fundamentalist, instead of telling me that my concept of goodness is different from that of God, says, "Your concept of goodness is no different from that of God; you two mean exactly the same thing by the term. It's just that God *knows* what is good better than you. If you had more *knowledge* of all the factors involved, then you would approve of eternal punishment!"

Now, this defense strikes me as thoroughly irrefutable! For example, suppose it should turn out (for some weird reason or other) that if the damned didn't suffer, then the totality of suffering in the universe would be much greater! In other words, God caused (or allowed) the sufferings of the damned simply to prevent far greater sufferings. If this were the case, then of course I would approve of eternal punishment—I would indeed say it is *good* of God (in *my* sense of the word "good") to do this. Of course, I could be extremely disappointed that God couldn't have created a better universe—a universe in which *all* suffering would ultimately cease—but then how could I blame God for doing something whose ultimate purpose was to relieve suffering? Yes, if my present conjecture is correct, then eternal punishment is certainly compatible with (in fact implied by) the goodness of God (goodness as *I* understand it).

But I don't believe that many (if any) hard Christians would accept this conjecture as at all plausible. (And I agree with them here; the conjecture is only logically possible, not *plausible!*) They would be more likely to say, "No, no! God doesn't punish the wicked in order to prevent the sufferings of others; it's that the sufferings of the wicked is *good in itself*—it is God's justice." Moreover, suppose the hard Christian adds, "I mean that the suffering of the wicked is a good in itself in *your* sense of the word 'good.' It's just because of your lack of knowledge that you fail to realize that it is good."

I find this the most intriguing and baffling position of all! (I never heard this position actually taken; I'm simply trying to make as strong a case for hard Christianity as I can.) What I find so intriguing in this position is that I don't see how it can possibly be refuted, and yet I find it psychologically impossible to believe! It also raises the very same difficultly as before: If my further knowledge would cause me to realize that eternal punishment of the wicked is good for some reason that I as a mere mortal cannot understand, then *anything* becomes possible! For example, it could be that everybody—good, bad, and indifferent—deserves eternal punishment. (As a matter of fact, many hard Christians have believed that everyone born under Adam's sin *does* deserve eternal punishment, only God in His mercy spares some.)

It all really boils down to this: If a person cannot trust either his own reason or his own moral sense, then anything becomes possible. As one Chinese scholar (I forgot who) wisely said, "The Chinese have too much common sense to believe that they are fundamentally evil, for they would reason that if they were, then their judgment as to what was good and evil would be unreliable."

To summarize: Suppose that eternal punishment is a reality and that God eternally punishes the wicked on no other grounds than that they *deserve* it. Can such a God be good? Of course, He can be good in God's sense (anyone, no matter how evil, can be good in his own sense), but the question is whether such a God can be good in the only sense that I, a mortal, can understand the term. Some claim that this is logically impossible, but I don't see why it is. Of course, I find it implausible, but that's not the same thing as logically impossible. In the last analysis, I can only hope and have faith that it is false.

The Psychology of Hard Christianity

One reason I am so concerned about hard Christianity is this: Many thinkers have strongly expressed the opinion that nothing could drive a person to hard Christianity other than sadism. Hard Christians, of course, refute the charge. I would like to be as fair as possible to the hard Christians and try to examine to what extent the charge is warranted.

As I see it, a hard Christian could take one of two possible attitudes toward eternal punishment:

1. "Unrepentant sinners are obviously so evil that they *deserve* eternal punishment. God is right in putting them in hell. I'm glad God does this; the sinners *deserve* it!"

2. "Personally, I find the idea of eternal punishment quite horrible, but I trust that God is good and knows what He is doing. However, I may feel about the matter is quite irrelevant: I simply have complete faith in the infinite wisdom and goodness of God."

Attitudes (1) and (2) strike me as so different, that they seem almost like different religions! Perhaps I should subdivide hard Christians into two groups—Group I and Group II (depending on whether their attitude is that of (1) or (2).

It is extremely difficult for me to see those of Group I as anything other than sadists—except for *one* factor that I will shortly consider. As to those of Group II, I don't see anything at all sadistic about them! They may be misguided; they may be totally wrong in their beliefs in eternal punishment; but I cannot see anything necessarily *sadistic* in their attitudes!

Coming back to those of Group I, is there *nothing* I can say on their behalf? Nothing that I can say that might save them from the charge of sadism? Yes; there *is* one thing I can think of—namely, that the reason they take that attitude is that they are terribly frightened that, if they don't, then they themselves will be damned! If that be true, then their motive is not sadism, but simply *self-protection!* This I can forgive (though not completely, since they are leaving the others—the sinners—in the lurch!).

Of course, there are also those Christians who would take what they would call an "objective" attitude toward the matter and say, "I don't believe that my belief in hell—and that it is willed by God—is due either to sadism or fear. I simply believe in the Scriptures, which, to my mind, clearly imply that the doctrine is true."

Ultra-Hard Christianity

Now, let me say a little more about ultra-hard Christianity. I have already mentioned Jonathan Edwards. Here are some more of his juicy bits: "The sight of hell torments will exalt the happiness of the saints forever.... It will make them more sensible of their own happiness.... A sense of the opposite misery in any case greatly increases the relish of any joy or pleasure" (quoted in Unamuno 1925, p. 384). (I am reminded of the witticism of a certain intellectual. He said, "It is not enough to succeed. One also needs a friend who fails.") I think, at this point, Jonathan Edwards has pretty well hurt his case—certainly, according to the general conscience of today. What he said amounts almost to a reductio ad absurdum argument against hard Christianity.

Then, there was his contemporary Samuel Hopkins, who added the following choice morsels:

> The smoke of their torment shall ascend up in the sight of the blessed for ever and ever, and serve as a most clear glass always before their eyes to give them a bright and most affecting view. This display of the divine character will be *most entertaining to all who love God,* and will give them the highest and most ineffable pleasure. Should the fire of this eternal punishment cease, it would in a great measure obscure the light of heaven, and put an end to a great part of the happiness and glory of the blessed. (ibid.)

I was particularly interested in the idea that the more one loves God, the more pleasure one will take in the sufferings of the damned. I wonder if there has existed—or now exists—any Christian sect which goes so far as to believe that unless one *does* take great pleasure in the sufferings of the damned, one cannot be saved? Would even Edwards or Hopkins have believed that?

In opposition to hard Christianity—and especially ultra-hard Christianity—the Congregationalist Reverend Leonard Bacon, D.D., wrote the following in 1888:

> My mind has been revolted by the tone and temper with which this doctrine [eternal punishment] is commonly set forth, whether in theological treatises or in preaching. I find it impossible to share the admiration so often expressed for the calm composure with which Jonathan Edwards quietly delivered his soul of that frightful sermon on "Sinners in the Hands of an Angry God," while listeners were crying out, or falling convulsed or clinging in terror to the columns of the church; a less complete self-command would have seemed more desirable in the preacher. The gross anthropopathy which describes the fury of God against the sinful in terms of the most savage and unchristian of human passions, has seemed to me to be imputing to the All-Holy that which is "unlikest God within the soul." The excited declamations with which, safe behind the pulpit breastwork, the flushed revivalist used to hurl the warnings of this fury into the midst of the people was only less painful to the reflection than the serenity of Edwards.

Now comes the particularly interesting part!

> But the argument with which it was sought to comfort bereaved and broken hearts, agonized over the thought of tortures multiplied from age to age throughout endless ages and ages, upon those whom they most tenderly love, by the promise that they should themselves experience so deep an inward change that the spectacle of the anguish of their friends, their children, would enhance the raptures of their heavenly bliss—let me refrain from characterizing it. (quoted ibid., pp. 119–20)

The author then says in a footnote that he does not distinctly remember having heard this line of argument used in the pulpit, but that he is credibly informed of a conspicuous living evangelist who used it with lively illustration and noticeable effect in his sermons to children. He also says that it has a very important place in the systems and sermons of the earlier Edwardsian systematizers and preachers.

It would be a mistake to believe that ultra-hard Christianity is something purely of the past! There are many revivalists today on television who seem to have a great time describing the hideous tortures of hell! Also, I know a Fundamentalist couple who are close friends with a Catholic couple and who are worried about their salvation. Moreover, the Fundamentalist wife said to the Catholic couple, "If you do not convert, I will take the utmost pleasure in your future tortures in hell." The husband was not willing to go that far. (He is a hard Christian, but not an ultra-hard Christian.) I wonder if his wife is worried about *his* salvation.

Is ultra-hard Christianity logically inconsistent? I see no reason why it is. It seems to me to be *logically* possible—the ultra-hard Christians could be right and I wrong. It may be that if I were a really good person, I would take the utmost pleasure in the tortures of the damned—even those of my loved ones. Pleasant thought!

Is ultra-hard Christianity necessarily motivated mainly by sadism? It seems extremely difficult to believe that it is not! A valuable clue here is Edwards's statement "A sense of the opposite misery in any case greatly increases the relish of any joy or pleasure." Or is it possible that even the ultra-hard Christians feel as they do because of their fear that, if they don't, they will be damned? Is ultra-hard Christianity a logical outcome of hard Christianity? I shall now consider this.

Is It?

Well, let us see if any light can be thrown on the question of whether ultra-hard Christianity is a necessary logical outcome of hard Christianity.

Argument for: God is good, and so He surely takes pleasure in His own good works. Now, eternal punishment is one of His good works—one of His best, in fact—and so He surely takes pleasure in it. Hence, those who are good—those who share in God's goodness—will share in His pleasure of eternal punishment.

Counterargument: Although God is good, and eternal punishment is good—as every good Christian knows—it does not necessarily follow that He takes pleasure in it! For example, a person may submit to a painful medical treatment because he knows that it is good for his health, but he certainly doesn't take *pleasure* in it! And so it is with God. Indeed, He may even be terribly *pained* by the suffering of the damned in hell; nevertheless, He *must* do it for the sake of justice and righteousness!

And so, we should worship God all the more for his great nobility and self-sacrifice! Just think: He is sacrificing even His *own* happiness for the cause of justice and righteousness!

Umpire's Decision: Of course, God is good, and eternal punishment is therefore good, otherwise God wouldn't permit it. The counterargument above is correct in that it does not follow that God necessarily takes pleasure in it. But to say that He takes pain in it is going too far! God doesn't let good beings suffer (except in the one case of the crucifixion), and since God is good, He therefore doesn't let Himself suffer (again, except for that one exception). Therefore, God takes neither pleasure nor pain in the sufferings of the damned—He is totally indifferent.

More on Hard Christianity and Sadism

I once frankly told a Fundamentalist friend that I believed that sadism is the main motivation for belief in the whole doctrine. He calmly replied, "You really believe that I and those of my faith behave more sadistically than others?"

I certainly do *not* believe that! Historically, hard Christianity has certainly led to more hideous persecutions than any other faith. (I am thinking of things like the Spanish Inquisition, the countless slaughters due to Calvin, and the torturing and burning of witches.) But I would not say that twentieth-century hard Christians *behave* more sadistically than others. Indeed, I can think of a reason why they might behave *less* sadistically.

Let us consider even the extreme case of ultra-hard Christians —those who take positive *pleasure* in the thought of the sufferings of the damned. Here they are enjoying their sadistic fantasies to their hearts' content, but these fantasies are actually hurting nobody! It may well be that their sadistic energies are thus being drained off and hence they might have *less* sadistic energies for the affairs of this life than do normal people.

A Curious Fact

A most remarkable thing about the hard Christians is their insistence that eternal punishment arises purely out of *God's love!* Love for *whom,* may I ask? I guess their only possible answer is "Love of justice." Isn't it remarkable that God loves an abstract principle (justice) more than the welfare of sentient beings?

A cute incident: Once in a restaurant, a proselytizing group came up to me, and one of the girls said, "Jesus loves you!" I replied, "Oh boy! I'm sure glad that *somebody* does! I could use a little love at this point!" Some interesting questions now arise. I presume that the girl meant "Jesus loves you and wants you to be saved." My first question is this: Suppose she is right. Then during my entire lifetime, Jesus will love me and hope that I will accept him as my savior. But suppose that I die without accepting Jesus. After my death, will Jesus suddenly *stop* loving me? This is certainly *logically* possible, but strikes me as most remarkable!

A second (and more interesting) point: If Calvinist doctrine is true, then it is *impossible* that Jesus loves me *and* wants me to be saved! Why? Because, according to the doctrine, God knows in advance who will be saved and who will not. (Even though we have free will and can make our choices, God knows in advance how we will choose!) And so God already knows whether or not I will be saved, and so certainly Jesus must also know this! Since Jesus knows whether or not I will be saved, then it is impossible that he *wants* me to be saved! Yes, he could be *happy* that I am saved (if I am), but he can't *want* something if He already knows whether or not it will come to pass! Therefore (if Calvinism is true), it is absolutely impossible that Jesus both loves me *and* wants me to be saved!

Of course (still assuming that Calvinism is true), it is possible that the girl was right in saying that Jesus loves me—but if she is, that would imply that I *am* saved (otherwise Jesus wouldn't love me, would he?)

Two Faces of Jesus

What I call the *first* face of Jesus is best described by the following line of Walt Whitman: "Recall Christ, brother of rejected persons—brother of slaves, felons, idiots, and of diseased persons" (Whitman 1885, p. 173).

If that's all there were to Jesus, it would be fine! But there is also the *second* face of Jesus—the Jesus who threatens eternal punishment to those who don't accept him as their savior! Accept *which* of the two faces, may I ask? Suppose I accept the first face but not the second (which, in fact, is what I do). Is this enough to save me? Or must I accept both in order to be saved? If accepting just the first is enough, then I am saved. If I have to accept both, then I am not saved. It's as simple as that!

Postscript: I really do believe that these two aspects of Jesus have been responsible for an enormous amount of psychological confusion—amounting almost to schizophrenia! When proselytizers say, "How can you possibly reject such a wonderful being as Jesus—the best friend of the poor and oppressed and who gave his life to save you from eternal torment? How can you be so horrible?" When they say this, they totally forget that it is the *other* side of Jesus that is being rejected!

In my library I have side-by-side Bertrand Russell's *Why I Am Not a Christian* with a book by Frank Crane titled *Why I Am a Christian.* Both books are equally good—in fact, both are *very* good! Both are valid, but one-sided. Russell points out with perfect accuracy all the bad things about Christianity and ignores the good things. Crane points out all the good things and ignores all the bad things —or rather, he simply *rejects* the bad things. (For example, he does *not* believe in eternal punishment!) Crane makes quite explicit that his belief in Christianity has absolutely nothing to do with any hope of salvation or fear of damnation. I don't think he is even concerned with whether Jesus is the incarnation of God or not! He simply accepts Christ because he regards him as the sanest and wisest teacher who ever lived. Russell, on the other hand, makes quite explicit why he believes that Jesus was *not* the best and wisest man who ever lived.

Why Was Jesus Sorrowful?

We hear that Jesus so "sorrowed" at the sins of mankind. Why was he so sorrowful? Was his sorrow mainly for the *victims* of the sinners or for the sinners themselves? If the former, then I can understand it perfectly! But some would tell me that it was mainly the latter. Then I am somewhat puzzled! I take it that this then means that Jesus sorrowed at the horrible fate in store for the unrepentant sinners. Now, if *soft* Christianity is the truth, then again I can perfectly understand Jesus' sorrow—he is *unable* to help the unrepentant sinners. But if *hard* Christianity is the truth, then the situation becomes really puzzling! If God (Jesus) is so worried about the fate of the unrepentant sinners and is *able* to spare them, then He could do so easily enough *if He wanted to*. Then why doesn't He? Is it that He thinks, "How horrible their fate! I feel so sorry for them! However, I can't spare them without violating justice, righteousness and holiness—which are even more important!"

Poor God, if He feels this way! He must suffer enormously!

Postscript: If we consider ultra-hard Christianity, an even greater puzzle arises! I am now thinking of that version which holds that we *should* take pleasure in the sufferings of the damned, and that the more one loves God, the more pleasure one will take. Well, Jesus certainly loved God, didn't he? Hence Jesus must take pleasure in the sufferings of the damned. But doesn't this sound a *bit* unlike Jesus?

A Strange Thought

In the fourth Gospel, Jesus said, "My Father and I are one." Did he mean this literally? Later he says, "The Father is greater than I." Quite a contradiction, isn't it? And yet—

And yet I have the following strange thought: Isn't it possible that when Jesus made the first statement, he actually was the Father, and when he made the second, he wasn't? Why must it be an all-or-none matter? Why isn't it logically possible that at certain times an individual might be identical with God and at other times not?

More on This

OR: Isn't it possible that the spirit of God entered Jesus at certain times and left him at others? While the spirit was within him, then he *was* God, and when the spirit left him, then he wasn't. Is this really so out of the question? Many people have told me that the reason they ascribe divinity to Jesus is that they feel that no ordinary human could say the things that Jesus said. And I must say that many of these things do strike me as Godlike. But other things he said seem most un-Godlike (such as his reference to eternal punishment). So wouldn't my hypothesis explain this discrepancy?

Also, when he said, "Father, why hast thou deserted me?"—isn't it possible that when he said that the spirit of God really *did* leave him? Isn't it possible that God had his special reason for sometimes entering the body of Jesus and sometimes leaving it?

OR: Instead of speaking of the spirit of God entering and leaving the body of Jesus, perhaps it would be more realistic to say that at certain times Jesus attained full union with God and at other times not. At the times when he did, he could correctly say that he and the Father were one, and at other times not.

Assuming that there really is a God and that individuals really can attain union with Him (Her? It?), what I am suggesting seems quite reasonable, doesn't it? Of course, the idea is quite unorthodox, but does that necessarily mean it is false?

A Thought on Calvinism

There is one corollary of Calvinistic theology that strikes me as quite remarkable: According to Calvinist doctrine, God knew in advance of the creation of the world who would be saved and who would be damned. God *could* have created only those who were to be saved (and ultimately become angels) but preferred to also create those who were to be damned. This means that God *could* have created a universe which would ultimately reach the state where there would be no suffering at all—only God and angels enjoying themselves eternally—but He preferred to create a universe in which suffering would never cease (the suffering of the evil ones). And this must be a better sort of universe, otherwise God would never have created it.

My point is this: Suppose the Calvinists are right that it is better that the unrepentant sinner should suffer eternally than that he should not. This means that the present setup is better than one in which all unrepentant sinners would be ultimately forgiven. But why does this imply that the present setup is better than one in which there were no unrepentant sinners at all? God *could* have arranged this but evidently chose not to. Isn't this a bit puzzling?

Let me put the matter another way. All right, the Calvinists say that God cannot forgive the unrepentant sinner, since this would involve a violation of righteousness and justice. They also believe that God *could* have created a universe in which there is no eternal suffering and could have done this without any violation of justice!

Why didn't God do this? I guess the only answer the Calvinists can give is "It is not for us to question the ways of God." Well, even if that is so, it still remains extremely puzzling why a just universe in which there is eternal suffering is better than an *equally* just universe in which there is not.

Religion as a Consolation?

One of the "selling points" of Christianity is that it is claimed to be a religion of consolation. Now, this should be seriously questioned!

Christianity certainly has been a source of great consolation to some, but an equal source of terror to others. When someone is told by a hard Christian that his ancestors and many of his loved ones are doomed to eternal torments in hell, you can hardly expect him to be consoled! On the other hand, if one has been worried a good part of his life that *he* is destined for hell, but one day feels that he is saved, the feeling must afford him infinite relief, and so he is then "consoled."

In the famous controversy between the nineteenth-century agnostic Robert Ingersoll and the Christian apologist Dr. Henry Fields, Ingersoll saw Christianity as nothing other than a religion of terror, and Fields saw it as nothing other than a religion of consolation. Despite letters back and forth, neither side budged an inch. Obviously, both took a completely one-sided view of the situation.

The long and short of it is clearly this: One who believes that he is saved and who does not care (or maybe is even pleased) that others are not is bound to be highly consoled. But one who cannot stand the thought of even one being suffering eternally will obviously find in hard Christianity the very opposite of consolation.

The Fundamental Moral Question

Many Christian writers have claimed that even the smallest sin deserves eternal punishment. One well-known argument for this is that if you sin against a being, the better the being, the worst the sin—in fact, the evil of the sin is directly *proportional* to the goodness of the being that you sin against. Now, since God is infinitely good, then any sin against God is infinite and therefore deserves infinite punishment.

That is the argument. Do you accept it? Obviously some of you do and some of you don't. Those of you who don't, why don't you? Can you put your finger on just what is wrong?

Well, let us try to analyze the argument carefully. First of all, is it so obvious that the magnitude of a sin depends on the goodness of the victim? I grant that this assumption has *some* plausibility, but surely further proof is necessary! Is mugging a very good man worse than mugging a man who is not so good? This certainly seems questionable! Second, even if the first step is granted, why does it follow that the magnitude of the sin is *proportional* to the goodness of the victim? In fact, does the notion of proportionality make much sense in this context? Just what does it mean to say that one person is twice as good or three times as good as another?

Next, just what does it mean to sin *against God?* I don't know what sinning against a being means other than hurting that being unjustly. But is God capable of being hurt? Certainly not, according to traditional Christian belief. And so therefore the notion of sinning against God needs further explication. Perhaps this can be done; I don't know. But even if it can, how can it be established that any sin against God is of infinite magnitude? Assuming there really is a God and that God is infinitely good (whatever "infinitely" means in this context) and that there is such a thing as sinning against God and that it is really true that the magnitude of a sin is *proportional* to the goodness of the being sinned against, I guess that it *would* follow that any sin against God is of infinite magnitude. But there are many ifs involved!

Now comes the fundamental moral question: Assuming it is possible for a sin to be of infinite magnitude (whatever that means), does it deserve *infinite* punishment? In fact, does it deserve any punishment at all? Retributive ethics replies, "Yes, it deserves *some* punishment." But the overwhelming majority of even those who subscribe to retributive ethics regard it as morally outrageous that any being at all—the worst sinner conceivable—should deserve *infinite* punishment! The doctrine that a being could deserve eternal punishment might aptly be called *extreme* retributive ethics.

It seems to me that this doctrine is the ultimate basis of that which I am calling "hard Christianity." Could hard Christianity survive without it? I do not see how.

An Interesting Legal Question

I have a relative, C, who is a practicing Catholic. I have had many arguments with him about eternal punishment. His attitudes toward that are relatively liberal: He does indeed believe that eternal punishment is a reality, but he believes in the possibility of salvation outside the Church—he believes that even atheists can be saved if they lead good lives.

One day he brought a Fundamentalist friend, F, to the house. The conversation turned to religion. At one point, I asked the friend, "Are you worried about C's salvation?" He replied, "Yes." The situation struck me as almost laughable! Here is poor C, who (as he expresses it) lives continuously on the razor's edge between salvation and damnation. (He is worried that evil temptations might come his way in the future that he may be unable to resist.) And here is F who believes that he himself is definitely saved and who is afraid that C is not saved because he lacks sufficient faith.

As I understand it, F's position is the Lutheran principle that if a person has complete faith that God will save him, then God will, and if he doesn't have sufficient faith that God will save him, then God won't. (In other words, a person is saved if and only if he fully *believes* that he is.) And so F is worried that C's uncertainty as to his own salvation indicates insufficient faith in God, hence C may not be saved!

Now, let us suppose that Luther's thesis is right—that if a person believes that he will be saved, then he will be. I now raise the following question: Suppose I believe the following two propositions:

1. I will be saved.

2. Everybody will be saved.

Does my belief in (2) disqualify me from salvation? Many a Christian will reply, "Yes. This Universalist belief that everyone will be saved is a clear heresy. It is a sin to believe that."

But suppose I reply, "Even if my belief in (2) is a sin, I have so much faith in God that I believe he will save me even though I am committing that sin."

So, will I then be saved or won't I?

A Question of Semantics

To repeat an earlier point, when apologists for eternal punishment are asked how Christianity, which calls itself a religion of *love*, can sanction eternal punishment, one stock answer is "Love includes love of justice." An even more interesting answer that I have come across is "Love includes love of holiness and righteousness. These demand eternal punishment. Although love of sentient beings constitutes an important aspect of morality, holiness and righteousness constitute *the most important* aspects of morality."

I am reminded of a cute conundrum posed by Abraham Lincoln: If the tail of a dog were called a leg, how many legs would a dog have? The answer given to Lincoln was *five*. Lincoln replied, "No, the correct answer is *four*. Calling a tail a leg doesn't mean that it is one!"

I can similarly say that *calling* eternal punishment just, holy, or right doesn't mean it really is! I cannot see that these three nice-sounding labels when attached to eternal punishment make it one whit less wrong! Suppose I ask, "*Why* is eternal punishment just, holy, or right?" I guess the only possible answer is "Because God says so." And so the deadlock remains.

Down to Brass Tacks

Here, as I see it, is the heart of the matter: Let's assume with the orthodox Christians that the voice of Jesus was really the voice of God. (If this be false, then my present inquiry is pointless!) The key question, then, is: Did Jesus believe in eternal punishment, or didn't he? Some orthodox Christians believe he did, and other equally orthodox Christians (orthodox in that they do believe that Jesus is the incarnation of God) believe that he didn't. He certainly gave *hints* that he did, and it seems to me that the efforts of kind-hearted Christians to gloss this over are not very convincing. I'm very much afraid that *if* Jesus was the incarnation of God, *then* eternal punishment is a reality. (It is mainly for this reason that I cannot believe that Jesus *is* the incarnation of God—I cannot believe that a good God can allow eternal punishment.) But let me continue with the assumption that Jesus *is* the incarnation of God. Now comes the curious (almost paradoxical) fact: If Jesus did believe in eternal punishment, then it is impossible for me (and those like myself) to accept him. If Jesus didn't believe in eternal punishment, then I would have no difficulty accepting him—but then my acceptance or nonacceptance would be of little importance, since there would be no eternal punishment anyhow! Isn't this a curious deadlock?

Let me put the matter this way: Suppose I said, "I accept you, Jesus, if and only if you don't believe in eternal punishment." Now, suppose Jesus *does* believe in eternal punishment (and hence that eternal punishment is a reality), would Jesus *then* save me on the basis of this purely *hypothetical* acceptance?

To put my question as generally as possible, I would ask it this way: According to hard Christian doctrine, does one have to believe that eternal punishment is both real and good in order to avoid eternal punishment? That is the crucial question! If you answer "Yes," then I will admire you for your consistency, but I will of course not believe that you are right. (That is, I will believe that your answer is consistent with your total doctrine—in fact implied by it!—but I will not accept your total doctrine.)

If you answer *no*, then I will love you for your good-heartedness, but as a logician I would have to sadly point out that *yes* would have been the more consistent answer! My argument is briefly this: Since God is good and Jesus is the incarnation of God, then Jesus is good—and also never makes mistakes. Since Jesus indicated that there is eternal punishment, then there really is. And since God is good, then eternal punishment is good. And so if you believe that eternal punishment is not good, then you are doubting that God is good—hence you are not accepting Jesus as your savior. Hence you will be eternally punished.

Is there anything wrong with this argument?

A Dialogue

QUESTIONER: Now, let me understand this clearly: You say that since God is infinite, then any sin against God is a sin against an infinite being, hence deserves eternal suffering. Is that it?

CALVINIST: Yes, that is what we believe.

QUESTIONER: Then I am puzzled. By the same logic, wouldn't it follow that any good act toward God, no matter how small, is a good act toward an infinite being, hence is deserving of eternal happiness? Yet those of your persuasion never seem to mention this. Why?

CALVINIST: (after much thought) You do indeed raise a good point, and I can see why those of my faith have had difficulty in answering it. But it *can* be answered. My answer is simply that it is indeed true that even the smallest good act deserves infinite reward. However, it is simply impossible for an unsaved person to commit *any* good act whatsoever! The unsaved person is free to choose evil, but he has no freedom to choose good—even in the slightest degree. One cannot choose the good without supernatural help.

QUESTIONER: Now, just a minute! You mean to say that an unsaved person cannot lead a life of thorough devotion to the welfare of the human race and prove to be a great benefactor?

CALVINIST: No, I am not saying that. An unsaved person *can* do all these things, but if he is not saved, then in the last analysis, he is doing all this purely out of self-love. He does them merely because it gives *him* pleasure to be helpful to others.

QUESTIONER: Really, now, you sound exactly like the hedonists who try to explain away all so-called "altruistic" acts as disguised forms of selfishness. As they would say, "A person acts altruistically only because of the pleasure it gives *him* to act that way." You surely don't subscribe to this hedonistic doctrine, do you?

CALVINIST: Ah, there's where the genius of Jonathan Edwards comes in! He demonstrated that the hedonistic analysis of human behavior was absolutely correct *for the natural man!* It is only the *saved* man who is capable of acting from genuinely disinterested motives. This is extremely important to realize! And that's why I say that even though a good act on the part of an unsaved person would merit him an infinite reward, the fact is purely hypothetical, since only the regenerate man is capable of any goodness whatsoever. But I think we should now hear what our mediator has to say about all this. Tell us, what are your views on the matter?

MEDIATOR: Although I am not in the least bit convinced by your answer, I am struck by its ingenuity. It seems to me that your position is a perfectly consistent one and can never be disproved by any argument whatsoever. But mere consistency is no guarantee of truth.

CALVINIST: If my conclusion is false, then my argument supporting it must contain at least one false step. Can you point out to me exactly where the false step lies?

MEDIATOR: It is not so much a question of *false* steps; it is rather a matter of *unsupported* steps.

To begin with, the hedonists have never proved their point. They have analyzed one type of act after another, and in each case, regardless of how beneficial the act might be, they have shown how the act *could* be fully explained in terms of self-love. But they have never proved that this *is* the explanation. Psychological hedonism is simply a *theory*—a fully consistent theory, I believe (like solipsism), but it has hardly been established as a *fact!*

Incidentally, there is one aspect of the ethics of Immanuel Kant that is remarkably similar to that of the hedonists (though I doubt that Kant realized this)—namely, he believed that a helpful act motivated only by love and sympathy had no moral value; an act had moral value only if dictated purely by obedience to moral law. He said that an act motivated only by love and sympathy was a purely selfish one, since it was done only out of identification with the joys and sufferings of others. And so Kant thoroughly agreed with the hedonistic analysis of human behavior when applied to acts performed out of love and sympathy, but disagreed when it came to acts performed out of obedience to pure morality.

Frankly, I can't see why acts performed out of obedience to moral law can't also have a hedonistic explanation. Why can't it be that one performs them only for the *pleasure* of being moral—or perhaps to avoid the pain of a guilty conscience? No, the purely hedonistic position—though I do not accept it—makes more sense to me than Kantian ethics.

And I believe that Jonathan Edwards fully realized this! He did indeed believe that even acts performed in obedience to moral law were purely selfish *unless the performer of the act was already saved!* Now, what is wrong with their arguments? Well, as I said, the hedonists have never proved their point. Also, Kant never proved that acts performed out of mere love and sympathy were only another form of selfishness, nor that acts performed out of obedience to moral law were not. Finally, Edwards never proved that the hedonistic analysis was applicable to all acts of the unsaved man, nor did he prove that it was not applicable to the saved man. In short, these are all lovely and ingenious *theories*, but totally unsupported by any known *facts!*

Fear and Hope

I own a very curious book entitled *That Unknown Country; or, What Living Men Believe Concerning Punishment after Death.* It consists of the views of fifty then-living churchmen and theologians (mainly Protestants) on eternal punishment. About half the writers were hard Christians (but none were ultra-hard, as far as I could tell). I have not read all the chapters completely since there is much repetition (and also, the book is close to a thousand pages). I found chapter XVI of particular interest. The author was Reverend W. H. French, D.D., pastor of the United Presbyterian Church, Cincinnati, Ohio. He, more than any of the others, emphasized one particular angle which I believe must be psychologically extremely compelling to those who are highly suggestible. The title of the chapter is "The Nature of Sin is such that every transgression of the Law Deserves Death, and there is no Sin so Small but it deserves Damnation." He calls the doctrine of eternal punishment a "reasonable one." He says, "To ignorance, the picture of hell is revolting, but enlightened reason assents to the Word of God in all that it teaches respecting it, and in all that it is declared to be" (p. 327).

In company with many of the other authors of the book, he regards our very *conscience* as a testimony to the reality of eternal punishment. I doubt that this argument carried much conviction—even in the year 1888—since the majority of consciences even then bore no such testimony. But now comes a remarkable thing: He argues that our *fear* of eternal punishment is evidence for its reality! He puts the matter in the following haunting way:

> We can no more reject the lesson which an implanted appetite teaches than we can reject the entity of that appetite; hence we reason from the entity of the appetite to the existence of something to meet its craving. If there is an actual instinct of danger, we at once conclude that the danger is real. God did not clothe the terrapin with its coat of mail or encase an oyster in a house of shell without cause. When we see this provision of nature, we reason of a corresponding evil to be feared or an enemy to be shunned. Nor will it do to confine this to the natural world; it has a like application in the moral and spiritual world. Intelligences do not fear instinctively when there is nothing to be feared.

They have instincts that teach of real evils. There is a higher and nobler instinct in man than that which is in the animals. The instinct to escape danger is evidence of the danger to which the creature is liable. Neither beast nor bird secretes itself when there is no sign of danger. You may look quietly upon them and they, unconscious of your presence, remain in their state of exposure; but the sound of disturbance that indicates danger awakens fear, and they hasten to protect themselves and flee to a place of safety. Just so it is with man. The instinct of punishment after death is inwrought. All men have it. . . . They that have restrained prayer and have denied God and a future state of punishment, when there was no apparent or immediate danger, have been loud in their appeals to mercy when danger was near. This is truth so patent and well-known that it needs no instances to confirm it. (p. 328)

(The author then gives instances to confirm it.) I find the whole passage a masterpiece of horror—in a way it is a real work of art! Nevertheless, there are a few things that should be added.

In the first place, is it really true that the instinct of punishment after death is inwrought and that *all* men have it? I'm sure that most atheists and agnostics would stoutly deny that they have any such silly ideas. But isn't it possible that many such people *do* have such fears deep down, and they are simply *repressing* them? I believe that this *is* true and is far more frequent than is generally realized! (The fact that many atheists have converted on their deathbeds adds evidence for what I am saying.) After all, regardless of how intellectually enlightened the human race may be, hard Christian ideas have entered the general consciousness and, though consciously rejected by the more enlightened, may nevertheless enter deeply into their subconscious minds. And so I say that although it is probably an exaggeration to say that deep down *all* people have the fear of eternal punishment, it may well be that far more people have it than is generally realized. But suppose it were even true that *all* people have this fear—so what? This brings me to my second point.

The key message of the whole paragraph is that our *fear* of eternal punishment is evidence for its existence. On what does the author base this? Are there not such things as paranoia and hypochondria? Isn't the fear of eternal punishment a form of paranoia and a sort of hypochondria of the soul? Aren't there such things as irrational and morbid fears? The author doesn't even seem to consider this possibility.

And now comes a particularly important point that the author totally neglected: He has apparently forgotten that, in addition to fear, there is such a thing as hope! It is quite possible that a person might fear that there is such a thing as eternal punishment and at the same time hope that there is not. Now, why should a person's hopes be any less reliable as an indication of reality than his fears? From a purely rational point of view, neither fears nor hopes are a particularly reliable indication of what really *is*. But from a religious point of view, hopes are supposed to be at least as reliable as fears—in a way, even more so. There is, after all, the line in Corinthians: "Love casteth out fears."

I can imagine a hard Christian giving the following reply to what I have just said: "In the case under discussion you should follow your fears rather than your hopes, because your fears are from God, and your hopes are from the devil. God sends you these fears in order to save you. The devil sends you these false hopes in order to deceive you and hence to damn you."

This indeed is logically possible! But couldn't it just as well be the other way around? Isn't it possible that the belief in eternal punishment is from the devil—his purpose being to bring discredit on Christianity? The Jehovah's Witnesses, incidentally, believe just that, but a born-again Christian I know told me that the Jehovah's Witnesses is itself a devil's sect! Whom does one believe?

A remarkable thing which I wish more people would realize is this: According to many Calvinists, Lutherans, and possibly other Christian groups, it is all right—in fact good and laudable—to believe that one is saved, but it is evil and heretical to believe that *everybody* is saved! Isn't this remarkable?

The Key Question: How Would You Vote?

I

This question is addressed to those who do believe in eternal punishment. Suppose that when you get to heaven, God surprises you by saying the following:

> I know that there has been much controversy among Christians as to whether eternal punishment is or is not justified. Now, of course, I have my own ideas on the matter; nevertheless, I realize that this is-

sue is so important to you all, that I wish to respect *your* wishes on this matter. And so I have decided to let *you* vote on the issue. Each of you will please cast your vote as to whether I should or should not mete out eternal punishment to those who have died unrepentant sinners. I will abide by the majority decision.

My question is: Would you vote for or against? I would love to see a poll taken on this! I believe the results would be of enormous psychological significance!

II

Now, wouldn't it be interesting if, in fact, God *is* taking a poll right now! God, who can read all our thoughts, doesn't need us to literally *vote*. Why can't it be that God is waiting to decide on the question of eternal punishment—waiting until the end of the human race? He is then keeping count of how many of us *want* unrepentant sinners to have eternal punishment and will finally tally the results and act accordingly.

If this be so, then it means that it is up to *us* whether eternal punishment will or will not take place! Thus the controversies between the extremes of Christendom—say, Calvinism on the one hand and Universalism (which believes in everybody's ultimate salvation) on the other—these controversies amount to far more than a mere quest to *discover* the truth—they amount to our actually *legislating* the truth!

I often have the feeling that in emotionally charged controversies in general, each side feels deep down that he is *causing* his thesis to be true, rather than just *discovering* whether it is. In the last analysis, I wouldn't be surprised if many of the controversies between, say, hard Christians and Universalists simply boil down to the former *wanting* eternal punishment to be true and the latter definitely not. But I doubt that this covers all cases.

III

I would imagine that many hard Christians, if asked to state how they would vote on the issue, would simply refuse to do so. They would say, "The whole premise of God asking *our* opinion on the matter is so ridiculous that I refuse to give the question a moment's thought!"

Let me then make another try. Even if it is true that unrepentant sinners *deserve* to be eternally punished, it does not follow that God will actually punish them eternally. As all good Christians know, man does not know the limits to God's mercy, and so it is possible that God in His mercy might subject *no one* to eternal punishment. This is certainly a possibility, but it is far from an established actuality. One simply doesn't know.

Now, my present question is this: Do you *hope* that God in his mercy will forgive *everyone*? And by everyone I mean even those who have died fully unrepentant. Do you hope for this or not? Perhaps even this question you will refuse to answer. (You may well feel that it is somehow wrong of you to answer.)

I hope you see what I am driving at! What I am trying to find out is whether you believe in eternal punishment because you want it to be true, or because you believe that you are required to believe that it is true. To put the matter quite bluntly, do you want me, and those like myself, to be eternally punished or don't you? Of course, I realize that ideally you hope that I will convert and be saved. (I certainly credit you with that!) But suppose I *don't* convert, would you *then* want me to be damned or not? Or is it that you would say, "It's not that I *want* you to be; it's just that my religion says that you *will* be." To which I must reply, "But will you *approve* of my being damned?"

Let me put the matter even more painfully. Suppose someone does you a great service—say, he saves the life of your family at great risk to himself. Of course, you will be grateful to him for the rest of your life. But suppose he dies unconverted. Then all your appeals to God on his behalf will fall on deaf ears. God will reply, "I'm sorry; I know that his *works* during his lifetime were good and beneficial. Still, he has committed the unpardonable sin of not believing in me. Hence, he has to have eternal punishment."

Do you believe that you could still love God under those conditions? Or would you still say, "Yes, dear Lord; whatever pleaseth you, pleaseth me. Let *thy* will be done; not *mine*"?

IV

I wish now to tell you of some reactions I have had to the question How would you vote? One friend of mine—raised as a Jew, and now more or less agnostic—thought the whole business silly since, as he said, "You are considering a *second* degree unreality—

an unreality based on an unreality. First of all, the Bible is not true —that is the first unreality. On top of that, even if it were true, God would never base His decision on what *we* thought." I was quite intrigued by his concept of a second degree unreality—I had never come across this before. But I believe that his second objection was wrong: Assuming the Bible is true, God *has* sometimes been influenced by people. Didn't Moses, at one point, influence God to change his mind about destroying some of the Israelites?

Another person to whom I posed the question was a Greek Orthodox lady who taught Sunday school. She definitely believed in heaven and hell and didn't seem to be bothered by the latter. To my surprise, she did not believe that God was merciful—only that he was completely just. When I asked her whether or not she would vote for the abolition of hell, she thought for a long time and said, "That's extremely difficult to say!" She just couldn't make up her mind. She then said that the existence of hell was a matter of *logic*. As she put it, "You can't have a beginning without an end. There can't be something short without there being something long. There can't be a Heaven unless there's a Hell." (This is hardly *logic*; it's more like analogy, and a pretty bad one at that!)

Next, I asked this question to a devout Episcopalian—a musician and a wonderful person. To my surprise, he said that he would vote *for* eternal punishment! When I asked him why, he replied, "They [heaven and hell] are two sides of the same coin." (This was a bit reminiscent of the conversation I had with the Greek Orthodox lady!) I said, "You mean that the abolition of hell is *impossible?*" He replied, "Yes." I replied, "Then I am thoroughly confused! If the abolition is impossible, then the whole question of voting couldn't even arise!" Unfortunately, the confusion never got straightened out.

The most clever answer I ever got to my question was from an orthodox Catholic I met at the University of Notre Dame. He definitely believed in hell, and he definitely believed in retributive ethics. When I asked him who is benefited by the punishment of an evil person, he made no bones about saying that *nobody* is benefited, but that it is a good thing in its own right. Then I popped my question of how he would vote on the question of hell, and his reply was brilliant. He said, "I would vote for the abolition of hell, but this may well be an imperfection on my part." I reported this conversation to my friend the Lutheran minister, who said, "These Jesuits are *very* clever!"

A Dilemma Indeed!

HARD CHRISTIAN: You act as if *I'm* responsible for the existence of hell! I do indeed believe it's a reality, and I do believe it happens by the will of God—God is all-powerful and could prevent it if He wanted to. Why doesn't He? As Augustine said, because He *will* not. It's not for me to question the motives of my Creator!

DISSENTER: I have heard many hard Christian preachers say that the doctrine of hell is both reasonable and has Scriptural support. Do you believe this?

HARD CHRISTIAN: That it has Scriptural support is completely obvious to anyone who knows Scripture. Reasonable? Frankly, none of the arguments I have ever heard for its reasonableness have convinced me. Nevertheless, I do believe it is reasonable. Why? Not because I know the reason; it *must* be reasonable since God ordains it and God wouldn't ordain anything unreasonable.

DISSENTER: But doesn't it *bother* you—the thought of people suffering forever in hell?

HARD CHRISTIAN: Yes, to tell you the truth it does! I don't believe it *should*, since it is wrong to be bothered by anything God does, but I am a weak human and cannot help being bothered by it. I know this is a sin, but can only hope and pray that God in His mercy will forgive me for it.

DISSENTER: Would you like it if God *cured* you of this sin? Would you really prefer to get to the state that you were no longer bothered by the sufferings of those in hell?

HARD CHRISTIAN: Oh, please don't ask me such horribly painful questions! Whatever answer I give seems wrong! On the one hand, I am horrified by the idea of being in such a state! On the other hand, I know that it is *evil* of me *not* to want to be in such a state. One *should* be happy with the will of God!

DISSENTER: I'm sorry; I shouldn't have asked you that!

HARD CHRISTIAN: But now, I'd like to get to your problem. Why are you so troubled by this all? You don't believe in our religion.

DISSENTER: That last is not strictly true! I'm very much afraid that there really may be a God and an eternal hell. My difference from you lies more on a moral than a factual level. I simply cannot believe that such a God can be good! But it's my very doubt that such a God can be good that will lead to my damnation! At least, that's what I'm afraid of.

HARD CHRISTIAN: Then why don't you pray to God to help you? Why don't you pray for Him to guide you to the realization that His overall scheme (which includes hell) is really good after all?

DISSENTER: For essentially the same reason that you don't want to get to the state that you are no longer bothered by hell! The only difference is that you believe that you are *wrong* in not wanting to be in that state, whereas I believe that I am *right* in not wanting to accept the goodness of a God who allows a hell.

HARD CHRISTIAN: Then what is your problem?

DISSENTER: My fear that I will be damned for my attitude!

Discussion: It seems to me that the poor dissenter is in a most hopeless position! Whatever he does is wrong! If he doesn't pray for guidance, then he will be damned (so he fears). If he does pray, then he is afraid that he may *falsely* accept God's goodness in allowing a hell, which won't mean that he will be damned, but that he will morally deteriorate in sanctioning an unspeakable evil!

Collective Salvation

Now I come to one of my main points: How would you like a religion that holds the following: When the day of judgment comes, God takes the average of the good and evil deeds of the entire past of the human race. If the average is high enough, then *everybody* gets saved! If the average is too low, then everybody gets damned.

How would you like such a scheme? You realize what this means: Every good act of yours will serve to save not only you, but everybody else as well. And every evil act of yours will threaten to damn not only you, but everybody else. Do you feel that people would act better or worse than under the scheme of individual salvation?

I would like to take a large statistical survey of people's reaction to this idea—I think the results would be most illuminating! So far, I have asked only a few people, and most of them prefer the idea of individual salvation. The first person I asked was a practicing Episcopalian. She replied, "I wouldn't like that at all! I think my chances would be much less!" Her reaction interested me for two reasons: (1) She immediately thought only of herself; (2) she evidently believed that she was a better person than the average human being. (I wonder if the majority of people think of themselves as better than average?)

The second person that I asked was an agnostic—closer to atheism than theism. She was brought up as a Catholic, but left the church long ago. She believes that the whole idea of salvation and damnation is complete nonsense, but the interesting thing is that she was extremely *irritated* with my idea! I replied, "Is it too *socialistic* for you?" She replied that she couldn't see any connection with socialism. To me the connection is obvious!

Let me digress for a moment and say a little about socialism. In many ways I *am* a socialist—more properly a social democrat. But there is one thing about socialism—or more properly about what is called "communism"—that I cannot and will not tolerate: namely, the idea that individuals should be *servants* of the state—or, to put it otherwise, that each individual should "subordinate his will to society." No, I regard the state as the servant of the individuals, not the individuals as the servants of the state! The idea that each individual *subordinates* his will to society fills me with horror! (In fact, I have always been allergic to the word "society.") Surely one can have a socialistic state without this horrible philosophical undercoating! To me, the idea is not submission of one's will to the state, but to live harmoniously with others. A mere change in terminology, you will say? No, to me the difference in wording reveals a profound psychological difference of attitude.

Curiously enough, the next person I interrogated was a socialist. He found the question very interesting, and, to my great delight, he said that he would vote for collective salvation.

Next, I asked a young "yuppie." His immediate reaction was strongly negative. The first thing he said was, "I hate anything collective!" But—to my surprise—as the conversation progressed, he at one point said, "I'm beginning to find this idea of collective salvation more and more interesting!"

Next, I was with a group of people, most of whom were Unitarians, but one Catholic was present. I proposed my scheme of collective salvation. The Unitarians seemed quite pleased with the idea. The Catholic said solemnly (but good-naturedly), "Oh! Oh! That's a dangerous religion! That's a *dangerous* religion!"

More recently, I proposed this scheme to a Catholic logician from Italy. (At least his background is Catholic; I don't know if he is still Catholic or not.) He was utterly delighted with the idea, and (I later heard) he went around telling it to lots of people.

There are really two questions about collective salvation that could be addressed to one:

1. Do you feel that *your* chances are better under collective salvation or individual salvation?

2. Forgetting yourself entirely, which of the two schemes would you prefer for the human race as a whole?

To me, the response to (2) is of greater interest. (The response to (1) would indicate only whether a person believes himself to be better or worse than the average human being.) Question (2) has more *moral* significance; the answer would reveal a good deal about the person's underlying moral structure. There are those who feel that collective salvation would be grossly unfair—why should the good suffer for the sins of the wicked? (Curiously enough, many of these same people are not disturbed by the idea that we should suffer for the sins of Adam!) Then there are those who are attracted by the idea of the human race rising or falling as a unit. Speaking personally, I would like to feel that whatever good I do will help not only me, but everyone.

Incidentally, for several years, I had the pleasant illusion that my idea of collective salvation was original; it's not! I just came across the following passage of Unamuno's in *The Tragic Sense of Life*:

> There are many, indeed, who imagine the human race as one being, a collective and solitary individual, in whom each member may represent or may come to represent the total collectivity; and they imagine salvation as something collective. As something collective also, merit, and as something collective sin, and redemption. According to this mode of feeling and imagining, either all are saved or none are saved; redemption is total and it is mutual; each man is his neighbor's Christ. (Unamuno 1889, p. 250)

Collective Salvation II

Suppose that the scheme of collective salvation described in the last piece is true. Then there is indeed an urgency in our behavior, because if not enough of us lead good lives, then all of us are lost. However, in this religion (if it can be called such) there would be no urgency in *belief*. If the religion were true, then it would not be necessary for any of us to believe it in order that we all be saved; it would only be necessary that enough of us *act* well.

I now would like to consider a second version of the scheme in which belief plays the crucial role. What I am about to propose is a socialized version of Luther's scheme of individual salvation. We recall Luther's idea that if a person has faith that God will save him, then God will—otherwise God won't. Well, here is my socialized version—my second scheme of collective salvation:

> If enough people believe God will save all of us, then He will. Otherwise He won't.

Obviously, under this scheme, *belief* rather than action is the crucial thing—we need enough people to have faith in order that we all be saved.

But now comes a very interesting *logical* problem (one closely related to the mathematical theory of common knowledge being developed today and which appears to have important applications in computer science) which I can only briefly discuss.

Let us suppose that all of us accept the above scheme. On what basis should we then believe that God *will* save us? The only way that He will is if enough of us *believe* that He will. Hence, for me to believe that He will, I must have enough faith that *others* will believe that He will. But others reason as I do, so for them to believe that God will save us, each of them must have faith that others will believe that. Therefore, for me to believe that God will save us, I must believe that others will believe that others will believe that! I must then carry this one step further—and one step further than that—and so on ad infinitum!

In short, even believing the scheme, I cannot see any *rational* evidence to believe that God will save us. Here a leap into faith is necessary! But not only faith in God, but faith in other human beings —faith that enough of them will have faith!

Meeting with a Born Again Christian

I was in a diner-type restaurant reading a book with the word "philosophers" in the title and came across something humorous to the effect that if God had created no sinners, He would have saved Himself a lot of trouble in trying to save them! I laughed heartily at this, and a man from an opposite table (who evidently had excellent eyesight) said, "It's interesting that something funny can be found in a philosophy book." I walked over and joined him and told him what I had read. He then asked me what I thought about salvation and told me that he was a born again Christian.

This was the first born again Christian I had ever met (or rather, the first person I ever met whom I *knew* was a born again) and I was delighted, since I had recently been reading William James's great book *The Varieties of Religious Experience* and was fascinated with the whole idea of the twice born. I soon asked his attitude about hell. He said, "Oh, I hate to think about it!" I said, "Yes, but do you believe it exists?" He said, "Yes, but I hate to think about it!" I asked him, "Then do you think you could be happy in Heaven knowing that others are eternally suffering in hell?" His answer was most unusual. He said, "Oh, I'm quite sure that when we get to Heaven, we won't know about hell—the knowledge will be taken away from us."

I was really stunned by this! I didn't know whether to praise him for his abhorrence of hell or to berate him for being willing to callously close his eyes to suffering. (Of course, I did neither.) Anyhow, this was the first person I had ever met who believed in hell and was pained by the idea.

He told me that he was formerly Greek Orthodox, but his real conversion came when he left what he characterized as "the happy family" and became an evangelist in a faith close to that of Billy Graham's. In personality, he seemed extremely relaxed, not at all uptight about his ideas—very human, very warm, and with an excellent sense of humor. (If being born again does this, there is something to be said for it!)

At one point, I said something that I believe may have been unkind. I said, "Here we are speaking as friends. Doesn't it bother you knowing that you are saved and I am not?" To my surprise, he replied, "Who said you are not saved? Jesus may call you any day!"

Postscript: Speaking of unkindness, there is one constant unkindness of which I have been guilty. Whenever I have met a hard Christian, I could not resist saying, "The difference between you and me is this: If God puts me in hell, then you will be on God's side, not on mine. But if God were to put you in hell, I would be on your side, not on God's!"

Of course, what I say is true. The unkindness consists not in its untruth, but in my saying it. It is really tantamount to saying, "You see how much kinder I am than you!" I beg the forgiveness of all to whom I have said it.

Fear and Love of God

There is one lay revivalist preacher (at least I believe he is not ordained) who lectures frequently in the open air on the campus of a Midwestern university, when the weather is good. His audience consists mainly of students. I recently passed by a group and heard the preacher saying something about fear of God. One of the students protested and said, "The idea is to *love* God; not *fear* Him!" The preacher replied, "I both love God and fear God." The student replied, "I do not *fear* God." The preacher replied, "Do you know why you don't fear God? The reason is that you are *stupid!*"

Many of the students got quite upset by this insult, and one yelled back, "Is that a Christian thing to do—to call your neighbor *stupid?*" The preacher, who is quite knowledgeable about the Bible, replied, "I have Scriptural support for what I am saying!" and then opened the book to a chapter in Jeremiah and read: "Anyone who does not fear God is stupid and a fool!" A student then said, "But you are not God; what right do *you* have to call someone stupid?" The preacher replied, "If God says someone is stupid, then I have the right to agree with Him." (Not a bad comeback!)

As I see it, the upshot of all this is the following: *If* the Bible is correct, then the student in question must be stupid. However, it was obvious from other remarks of the student that he is *not* stupid. This then only adds confirming evidence that the Bible is not always correct. But this is really a side issue.

I then asked the preacher two questions (prefacing them with a statement that they were not meant as criticisms, but that I was genuinely interested in his attitudes). First, I asked whether he believed that God was unwilling or unable to save the unconverted. To my great surprise he said, "God wants everyone to be saved. But he is *unable* to save those who don't turn to Him."

This, then, classifies him as what I am calling a *soft* Christian. But when I asked him whether when he got to heaven and was given the option of voting whether the unconverted should be eternally punished or not, he said that he would vote *for* their eternal punishment. This sounds more like a hard Christian, doesn't it?

The dilemma is this: If it is really true that the unconverted will suffer eternal punishment, then my deceased parents, my family, my best friends—all those I dearly love—are scheduled for eternal damnation. If God *wants* this, if He is the *cause* of this, then of course I would fear God, but I would find it impossible to love Him—He would then be our worst enemy. On the other hand, if God did His best to help my loved ones, but was unable to, then the *cause* of their damnation would be outside God. In that case, I would love God for trying to help, but would have no reason whatever to *fear* Him. (Why would I fear a friend?) What I would then fear is whatever it is (something outside God) that was the *cause* of damnation.

I think it is high time that Christians who believe in eternal punishment should get together and decide once and for all whether God is unwilling or unable to help those who have died unconverted. Upon this answer depends whether the rational thing to do is to fear God or to love God. I don't see how one can have it both ways. I believe that the lack of unanimous decision on this matter is causing enormous psychological confusion!

Retributive Ethics

I believe that retributive ethics is the real heart of the matter! Retributive ethics holds that doers of evil *deserve* to suffer. The thoughts of those who support this doctrine run something like this: "An evil act destroys harmony. The only way to restore the harmony is that the evil-doer suffer in return." Retributive ethics is the basis of vendettas, family feuds, wars, and partly (but not wholly) our criminal justice system.

A graduate student in philosophy, who prides himself on his rationality, once complained to me of the *irrationality* of a friend of his who once told him, "Even if I could be completely convinced that capital punishment is quite ineffective as a deterrent, I would still be for it. I believe that murderers *deserve* to be executed." And I replied, "And I am what you would call irrational in the *opposite* direction. If I were convinced that capital punishment was most effective as a deterrent, I would still be heartily against it. To me killing a man in cold blood is sheer savagery." He replied, "Yes, you are equally irrational!" (Incidentally, the idea that rationality has anything to do with this strikes me as utterly ridiculous!)

I said before that retributive ethics is only *part* of our system of criminal justice, the reason being that our system justifies the punishment of criminals on four grounds: (1) keeping the criminal off the streets, (2) deterring others from crime, (3) possibly reforming the criminal, and (4) righteous retribution.

To my way of thinking, (1) is the best reason for the existence of jails; (2) may also have some validity, but this is somewhat questionable; (3) is even more questionable (I *wish* it were true, but I'm afraid it is very doubtful!); as for (4), I regard that as horrible!

As you see, I do *not* support retributive ethics! Someone once said to me, "You mean that if someone deliberately injured someone you love, you would not hate him and wish him harm?" I replied, "I'm sure I would hate him—certainly at first—and I might well *feel* vengeful and I might or might not *do* him harm. But even if I wreaked my vengeance, that does not mean that I would *approve* of either my feelings or my act. I am no saint and I have no illusions that I am free from such feelings, but that does not mean that I approve of them. How I would feel and how I would act are totally irrelevant. The fact is that I believe that vengeance is a bad thing." She replied, "Is it that you believe that vengeance should be left to the Lord?" I replied, "No, no! I believe that a *good* Lord would never have said, 'Vengeance is mine,' but would have said, 'Vengeance is nobody's'! He would have added, 'The solution is not vengeance, but enlightenment.'" (This is *my* religion!)

Someone else once asked me, "Are you against retribution on the grounds that we have no free will and are hence not responsible for our acts?" I strongly replied, "That has absolutely nothing to do with it! I happen to believe that we *do* have free will and that when we act evilly, we *choose* to do so. Still, I don't believe that retribution is the appropriate response—whether from man or God!" (Again, this is *my* religion!)

Obviously, no one can possibly believe in eternal punishment unless he accepts retributive ethics. If one does not accept retributive ethics, how could he possibly believe in eternal punishment? But to reject the belief in eternal punishment, one does not have to be so drastic as to reject retributive ethics altogether! There are many Christians who believe that all evil *deserves* punishment, but that no evil deserves *eternal* punishment.

Postscript: I was once with a group, and the question came up whether someone as evil as Adolf Hitler deserves eternal punishment. Two of the members got extremely excited and shouted, "Absolutely! I would wholeheartedly put Hitler in hell forever!"

Then one of them added, "And I would add Ronald Reagan! He is doing as much harm as Hitler!"

I was somewhat amused by the savagery of their response, since neither of the two members are particularly evil. Furthermore, I believe that in a certain sense, their responses were not very accurate. If it actually came to a showdown and God asked either of them, "Should I really put Hitler in hell?" it is possible that each might answer *yes*, but I'm certain that if either one of them had to *watch* Hitler's agonies in hell for a minute or two, they wouldn't be able to stand it; they would cry, "All right, God. Enough!"

More on Retributive Ethics

On a more personal note, I firmly believe that all of us—the best of us!—have cruel and sadistic tendencies; that is part of our animal heritage. And the one socially acceptable outlet for our sadistic needs is retribution. I cannot fault a person for *feeling* retributive— that is only natural, as I have indicated. I fault only the *approval* of retribution. I believe that retributive ethics is one of the main forces—if not *the* main force—that is holding back our civilization. I predict that as we become more civilized, the decline in retributive ethics, the decline in the belief in hell, the decline in the approval of capital punishment, the decline of war, the decline in crime—all these things will come to us hand in hand.

Karma

Retributive ethics is not the same as karma! According to karma, every evil deed you do will rebound on you sooner or later—in this life or another—and every good deed you do will benefit you sooner or later. It's not a question of your *deserving* to be punished or rewarded, nor is there any conscious agent who administers punishments and rewards—it's just part of the laws of the cosmos that things work that way. It is analogous to sticking your hand in a fire; the fire is not punishing you; it's just that fire burns—just as evil deeds harm the doer.

I am reminded of an incident I read in some book on Buddhism. Someone was once insulting a Buddhist sage, and the sage replied, "Insulting a holy man is like spitting up at Heaven. The spittle doesn't reach Heaven, but falls back in his face."

Karma, unlike retributive ethics, is not so much an ethical doctrine as a factual one. But to me it has far higher ethical value!

C. S. Lewis on Hell

The famous Christian apologist C. S. Lewis wrote a chapter on hell in his book *The Problem of Pain*. Much of it is remarkably illogical, considering the cleverness manifested by the author elsewhere, and I wish to point out some of the illogicalities and to answer a question raised at the end of the chapter.

About the doctrine of hell, Lewis says, "There is no doctrine which I would more willingly remove from Christianity than this, if it lay in my power. But it has the full support of Scripture and, especially, of our Lord's own words; it has always been held by Christendom; and it has the support of reason" (Lewis 1962, p. 106).

I have already indicated that I fully agree that the doctrine of hell has the support of Scriptures (regardless of what Jehovah's Witnesses and Seventh-Day Adventists say), but to say it has the support of *reason?* To continue with Lewis's passage:

> If a game is played, it must be possible to lose it. If the happiness of a creature lies in self-surrender, no one can make that surrender but himself (though many can help him to make it) and he may refuse. I would pay any price to be able to say truthfully "All will be saved." But my reason retorts, "Without their will, or with it?" If I say "Without their will" I at once perceive a contradiction; how can the supreme voluntary act of self-surrender be involuntary? If I say "With their will," my reason replies "How if they *will not* give in?" (pp. 106–7)

Now, for my first criticism: Lewis is quietly confusing salvation with self-surrender or "giving in." Of course, it is possible that God is such that He refuses to save anyone who doesn't "give in." But that doesn't mean that refusing to give in means refusing to be saved; it means refusing to do that which happens to be necessary for being saved! It would have been more honest had Lewis ended the passage instead "How if they will not be saved?" Now, that would have raised an interesting question! Would a good and merciful God save someone *against his will?* Again, this should not be confused with the totally different question of whether a good and merciful God would save someone who wants to be saved (as I believe everyone does) but who will not take the required steps. Also,

Lewis does not take into consideration those who don't "give in," not because they are rebellious and refuse to give in, but who simply regard the whole business as a myth and don't believe in any being to whom one is supposed to "give in." If one doesn't believe in God, it is silly to say that he *refuses* to give in to God!

Another thing I objected to was Lewis's regarding the business as a "game." If it is a game, it is certainly not one which we have agreed to play. Now, when Lewis says that if a game is played, then it must be possible to lose it, that is fine if one has *agreed* to play the game. But is it just to *force* one to play a game, whether he is willing or not, and then penalize him if he loses? I think there is more than an illogicality here; I'm afraid that there is a subtle bit of dishonesty (though probably not fully conscious).

A bit further on, the author again speaking of the doctrine of hell, says, "I too detest it from the bottom of my heart." And a bit later: "I am not going to try to prove the doctrine tolerable. Let us make no mistake; it is *not* tolerable." Then, it seems to me, Lewis spends the rest of the chapter trying to make the doctrine tolerable. Indeed, the very next sentence is "But I think the doctrine can be shown to be moral, by a critique of the objections ordinarily made, or felt, against it."

Now, really! If the doctrine is both reasonable and moral (as Lewis asserts), then why on earth should it be intolerable? How can Lewis think this way? The only explanation I can think of is that Lewis must be of two minds on the matter! It is obvious to me that he has enough kindness in his soul to be horrified by the idea, yet his religion requires him to believe it (As he says, it has Scriptural support—and there he is right.) I really do feel sorry for those who find Christianity attractive, hell repulsive, and who believe that Christianity implies the existence of hell.

In a good portion of the chapter, Lewis paints a portrait of a thoroughly detestable individual who rises to wealth or power by a continued course of treachery and cruelty, jeering at the simplicity of his victims and finally betraying even his own accomplices, and who has not the slightest pang of conscience, but enjoys life like a child. (A thoroughly unrealistic picture, by the way!) Lewis then asks whether in good conscience we could desire that such a man *remaining what he is* should be confirmed forever in his present happiness—should continue, for all eternity, to be perfectly convinced that the laugh is on his side?

It seems to me that Lewis is here asking the wrong question! Of course, I would want such a person to realize the horror of what he has done, regardless of how much temporary pain it may cause him, but that doesn't mean that I would want to see him suffer *eternally* for it! A bit later, Lewis says, "The demand that God should forgive such a man while he remains what he is, is based on a confusion between condoning and forgiving. To condone an evil is simply to ignore it, to treat it as if it were good. But forgiveness needs to be accepted as well as offered if it is to be complete: and a man who admits no guilt can accept no forgiveness."

At this point, Lewis sounds like a soft Christian rather than a hard one, doesn't he? If God is *unable* to forgive one who is unwilling to accept forgiveness, then this is soft Christianity—it is like the idea of the soft Christian girl I spoke of earlier, who said that salvation is a gift and that no one can force another to accept a gift. To tell the truth, it is difficult to classify Lewis as a soft or a hard Christian—I think he comes closer to the soft.

Another illogicality: At one point, Lewis suggests that maybe hell is not painful to those in it, but only seems horrible to those outside it—to those in heaven. Well, this is certainly a kind thought, but if it were true, then hell would no longer be intolerable! Please now, Dr. Lewis, you can't have it both ways: Do you believe hell is intolerable or don't you? Again, I can only say that Lewis *wishes* that the doctrine of hell is false, but his religion *requires* him to believe it is true.

The last paragraph of the chapter strikes me as quite deceptive:

> One caution, and I have done. In order to rouse modern minds to an understanding of the issues, I ventured to introduce in this chapter a picture of the sort of bad man whom we most easily perceive to be bad. But when the picture has done that work, the sooner it is forgotten the better. In all discussions of Hell we should keep steadily before our eyes the possible damnation, not of our enemies nor our friends (since both these disturb the reason) but of ourselves. This chapter is not about your wife or son, nor about Nero or Judas Iscariot; it is about you and me. (p. 116)

What I find so dishonest about this paragraph is that the central portion of the chapter was *not* about you and me; it was about some total psychopath that Lewis invented! Even if some reader saw some justification in such a psychopath's being in hell, it wouldn't mean that he would want you and me to be in hell!

And now, I wish to give an answer to a vital question raised by Lewis. In the next-to-the-last paragraph, he says:

> In the long run the answer to all those who object to the doctrine of hell, is itself a question: "What are you asking God to do?" To wipe out their past sins and, at all costs, to give them a fresh start, smoothing every difficulty and offering every miraculous help? But he has done so, on Calvary. To forgive them? They will not be forgiven. To leave them alone? Alas, I am afraid that is what He does. (ibid.)

Before answering the question raised, I wish to consider two little points. First, is it really true that one cannot be forgiven without his consent? I see no evidence for this and cannot believe it. Second, according to the parable of the sheep and the goats in Matthew, in which the wicked are sent away to everlasting *punishment*, does this sound like God "letting them alone"? At this point, what Lewis says does *not* have Scriptural support!

But now, for the main question: What am I asking God to do? My answer is simple: If God *is* able to relieve the sufferings of those in hell, then I would want Him to do so. If He is not able, and is not able to annihilate them, then there is nothing He can do now, but He should never have created them in the first place. How could a decent God possibly create any being if there was even the remotest chance that, by misuse of his free will, he would land himself in a situation in which he would suffer eternally?

And if any reader should ask me, "Who are you to question the ways of God?" I would reply that I am *not* questioning the ways of God—I am questioning some of the ways that certain religions *attribute* to God.

Postscript: Actually, C. S. Lewis has a much nicer attitude toward hell in an earlier book, *The Pilgrim's Regress.* Here, the "Black Hole" (another name for hell) doesn't bear the slightest resemblance to a place of punishment, but is simply a place where God keeps unrepentant sinners from destroying themselves further! In this frame of mind, Lewis is clearly a soft Christian.

A Final Word on Soft Christianity

I have indicated that I believe that hard Christianity has more Scriptural support than soft Christianity, but that soft Christianity was the more moral position. But actually, soft Christianity may have as many moral difficulties as hard Christianity—namely, the point considered earlier, that no moral God would ever create any being if there were any possibility that he would suffer eternally. Surely, no one believes that God *had* to create all the beings He created, does he? And so soft Christianity may be as immoral as hard Christianity after all!

And this leads me to the realization that soft Christianity is simply not a viable position! It not only has no Scriptural support (which hard Christianity has), but also suffers ultimately from the same moral difficulties (though they are less on the surface). No, at this point I am forced to the realization that the only rational alternatives are hard Christianity or the nonexistence of hell (assuming the existence of a good God). Here are my reasons:

Either it is good that some people suffer eternally or it isn't. If it is good, then a good God will see to it that it happens, in which case hard Christianity is the truth. If it isn't good, then a good God will see to it that there is no hell. I see no other possibility.

Luther's Defense

As I have indicated earlier, those who believe in hell and that hell is a good thing are of two types. The first consists of those to whom hell *seems* a good thing; for example, those who feel that unrepentant sinners *deserve* it—that God's justice *demands* it. The second type consists of those who are highly uneasy with the idea, but have to believe it anyhow, since their religion demands it.

An interesting example of the second type is a born again Christian whom I recently met. I asked him my usual question of whether he would vote for or against the abolition of hell, were God to ask him. He replied, "I would vote for the abolition, but God's justice demands the existence of Hell." So here is a clear case of an honest expression of a dislike of hell combined with a religious belief in its necessity. Another Christian to whom I asked whether he believed that hell was a good thing replied, "I believe that God's notion of goodness is better than mine." I found that honesty admirable.

Some apologists for hell try to justify it by *reason*, others by *faith*. Here is what Martin Luther said about hell and faith (as quoted by Aldous Huxley in his book *The Perennial Philosophy*):

This is the acme of faith—to believe that God who saves so few and condemns so many, is merciful, that He is just who, at his own pleasure, has made us necessarily doomed to damnation, so that he seems to delight in the torture of the wretched and to be more deserving of hate than love. If by any effort of reason I could conceive how God, who shows so much anger and harshness, could be merciful and just, there would be no need for faith. (Huxley 1945, p. 256)

This defense of hell strikes me as the most intelligent one I have seen. He abandons reason altogether in favor of faith! I think that in this situation, the abandonment of reason is the most reasonable thing one can do. The justifications of hell based on reason are really quite weak and unconvincing, whereas a justification based on pure faith seems to me to be irrefutable. Not that I for a moment believe it, but I see no way to refute it. Faith, no matter how sincere and well intentioned, is obviously no guarantee of truth, but I don't see how beliefs based on faith, however implausible they may be to whose who do not share them, can be disproved with certainty. And so, I say to those who wish to justify hell, regardless of whether they like the idea or not, their best strategy is not to try to justify it by reason, but to honestly say, "However I may feel personally about it is unimportant, since I am a mere mortal. The fact is that God wills it, and since God is infinitely good, then hell must be a good thing for reasons that I may not be capable of understanding."

That may well be their best defense. It is not essentially different from that of Luther, and as I have said, it seems to be irrefutable.

The Moslem and Jewish Positions

I know least of all about the Moslem religion, but as I understand it, Moslems are ahead of many Christian sects in their belief that even after one is in hell, if he sincerely repents and begs Allah to forgive him, he will be forgiven. Incidentally, a very bright and knowledgeable graduate student in philosophy of Mexican origin told me that some Catholic theologians have claimed that if one in hell sincerely repents, he will be let out, but it is psychologically impossible for one in hell to repent! This strikes me as funny. What a perfect Catch 22!

As for the orthodox Jewish position, many people have the erroneous view that Jews do not believe in an afterlife. This may be true for many Reformed Jews, but it is certainly not true for the Orthodox. Every Orthodox rabbi whom I have ever asked has told me that he does believe in an afterlife. I asked one Orthodox rabbi what percentage of Orthodox Jews, in his opinion, believe in an afterlife. He replied, "Most, if not all."

However, they do *not* believe in any *permanent* hell! According to their doctrine, after death, a person is either purifiable or he isn't. If he is completely pure, he goes straight to heaven. If he is not yet pure, but purifiable, he goes to a *temporary* hell until thoroughly purged and then goes to heaven. If he is not even purifiable, then he simply gets annihilated (as the Jehovah's Witnesses and Seventh-Day Adventists believe). Speaking personally, I certainly prefer this to the doctrine of eternal punishment, but it is still not as good as the viewpoint of the Hindus, Buddhists, and Christian Universalists, which is that *all* souls are moving toward perfection—none are lost along the way.

An Orthodox rabbi once told me that Orthodox Judaism does *not* subscribe to retributive ethics—that God never punishes you because you deserve it, but only to either purify you or teach you a lesson. He punishes you only for your own good. Is this really true, or is it just a modern version of Judaism? It certainly doesn't sound to me like the God of the Old Testament—but then again, I've read only the English translation, so I can't be sure. If it *is* true, then I would say that it is vastly superior to the retributive approach, but still not good enough. I believe that a truly good and wise God could find a better way of guiding us than by punishment!

The Swedenborgians

Here is a particularly kind-hearted approach: According to Emanuel Swedenborg, all punishments for evil are self-inflicted; God Himself never punishes! Indeed, God and His angels are constantly trying to alleviate the sufferings of the wicked, regardless of how low they have fallen.

When we die, the good and the evil ones are both welcomed by the inhabitants of the spiritual world, who try to render us every service they can. No one is questioned as to his former life, but he reveals it by the society he chooses and by his thoughts and actions. The wicked cannot stand the presence of goodness—the very atmosphere of God is poisonous and terribly painful to them. And so they voluntarily depart and set up their own colony in a place as far removed from the atmosphere of goodness as they can. This is their hell. Since they are all totally selfish, they are constantly hurting each other. (This sounds a bit like Earth, doesn't it?) But the angels of God are constantly going to the hell of the wicked, ministering to their sufferings and preventing them from hurting each other as much as possible. In short, hell is not a penal institution in which the inmates are tortured for what they have done; it is more like an insane asylum! Every provision that infinite mercy can suggest is taken to assuage the misery of the unfortunate inhabitants and make their pitiful condition as endurable as possible.

And now, enough about the dark subject of hell! Let us turn to brighter matters. Put another way, we have remained in Dante's Inferno long enough; let us now ascend to Paradiso!

III *Cosmic Consciousness*

Cosmic Consciousness

In 1931, H. A. Overstreet, professor and head of the Department of Philosophy and Psychology at the College of the City of New York, wrote the following in his book *The Enduring Quest:*

> In the year 1901, a remarkable book was published by a Canadian physician and psychiatrist of wide reading and penetrative originality. . . . And yet, it is significant to note that in the thirty years since Bucke published this remarkable work, practically nothing has been done in the investigation of the idea which he suggested. Nevertheless this idea is so obviously important that it would seem to merit instant attention. It is the idea that, inasmuch as evolution of life forms (including the psychological) continues, we have every reason to believe that a further form of our conscious life is already observable among us— in high degree among rare individuals, in lesser degree among most of us. The full emergencies into that further form, Bucke suggests, would naturally not be instantaneous—the whole of humanity leaping, so to speak, into a new order of being. As in all stages of evolution, we should expect a slight difference in one more happily circumstanced individual, then in a few others, then in more, until finally the new form would become widespread and secure. What he proposed is that we look about to see whether there are any outstanding examples among us of a form of conscious life which might properly be regarded as of a higher order than that with which we are familiar. This, he suggested, would not be a form totally discontinuous with our normal consciousness, but one which would already be adumbrated in the more significant process of our mental and emotional life. (p. 234)

Speaking of the great people whom Bucke cited as cases of Cosmic Consciousness, Overstreet says:

> Wherein lay the secret of their superiority? That is the problem to which Bucke addresses himself. His answer, whether true or false—

and we must remember that his book was a pioneering venture—is sufficiently arresting to call for our serious consideration. Studying the life histories of these men, he finds in all of them—sometimes in great degree, sometimes in less—a clearly marked phenomenon of consciousness. These men do not reason their way to conclusions, although reason—the search for truth—apparently played a part in preparation for their final insight. In every case they experienced what, for want of a better term, we might call *illumination*. (p. 238)

I am utterly amazed that *Cosmic Consciousness* is so little known today! It is still in print and available in paperback, yet hardly anyone to whom I have mentioned it has ever heard of it! I have already indicated that I don't believe that any religious or metaphysical system yet propounded is wholly true, but of all the ideas I have yet heard, that of Bucke (and shared by Edward Carpenter, of whom I will have much to say) strikes me as the best approximation to date. Besides, the ideas involved are intensely beautiful and inspiring. Significantly, the book is subtitled "A Study of the Evolution of the Human Mind."

The author, Dr. Richard Maurice Bucke, who lived from 1837 to 1902, was a Canadian physician and psychiatrist who had a distinguished medical career. In 1876 he was appointed superintendent of the Provincial Asylum for the insane at Hamilton, Ontario, and in 1877 of the London (Ont.) Hospital. He became one of the foremost alienists in this hemisphere and introduced many drastic reforms in treatment which, though considered dangerously radical at the time, are considered commonplace today. In 1882 he was appointed Professor of Mental and Nervous Diseases at Western University (London, Ont.), and in 1888 he was elected president of the Psychological Section of the British Medical Association, and in 1880, president of the American Medico-Psychological Association.

When Bucke's *Cosmic Consciousness* was first published in 1901, William James wrote to the author: "I believe that you have brought this kind of consciousness 'home' to the attention of students of human nature in a way so definite and unescapable that it will be impossible henceforward to overlook it or ignore it. . . . But my total reactions on your book, my dear Sir, is that it is an addition to psychology of first rate importance, and that you are a benefactor of us all" (Bucke 1956, vi). In my edition of the book, there is a new introduction by George Morely Acklom who, speaking of the above words of James, says:

This last half sentence seems to me even more important than Professor James' verdict as a philosopher and psychiatrist. It explains the continuing life and usefulness of Cosmic Consciousness, for I firmly believe that no understanding mind can form a real acquaintance with this book without experiencing a tremendous uplift and stimulation. . . . It opens a new door—to give us a vista of strange and wonderful possibilities. (ibid.)

I wholeheartedly agree with these evaluations. Uplifting and stimulating the book certainly is—as much as any book I have ever read. I was curious that Acklom said, "It explains the continuing life and usefulness of Cosmic Consciousness." Is it that the book was better known in the fifties than today? Probably, since there were eighteen editions by 1956. Acklom says further:

Cosmic Consciousness is a book very difficult to classify. This is due to the fact that Illumination or Ecstasy of which it treats, is generally thought to belong to the realm of Religion or Mysticism, or of Magic and the Occult—or even, by some ultra materialists, to the domain of insanity. In Christian Mysticism, Illumination is the acknowledged third stage of the mystic's progress, coming after the two preliminary stages of Awakening and Purification. In both Brahmanism and Buddhism it is the reward of long and rigid self-discipline and effort.

But to Bucke it had nothing to do with mysticism or formal religion, or with conscious preparation and intention. He was a student of the human mind, a psychologist and he treated Illumination from the standpoint of psychology, as a very rare but definite and recognizable mental condition, of which many well-authenticated instances are on record and available for examination. . . . He deduced (from analysis of past cases) that the human race is in the process of developing a new kind of consciousness . . . which will eventually lift the race above and beyond all the fears and ignorances, the brutalities and bestialities which beset it today. (Introduction, n.p.)

What is this Cosmic Consciousness? According to Bucke, it is a higher form of consciousness that is slowly but surely coming to the entire human race *through the process of evolution!* The mystics and religious leaders of the past were simply in advance of their time—they were evolutionary *sports.* According to the author, there are three stages of consciousness. First, there is the simple consciousness of animals, which recognizes the things about them, as well as their own limbs and bodies and knows that they are parts of themselves. Next comes the self-consciousness of humans, which is not only of external objects and of their own bodies, but is of themselves as distinct entities apart from the physical universe. Cosmic Consciousness is a third form which is as far above self-consciousness as the latter is above simple consciousness. Its main characteristic, according to Bucke, is "a consciousness of the cosmos, that is, of the life and order of the universe."

Having read the book thoroughly (and several times), I somehow doubt that this definition is very informative. Indeed, I'm not sure that *any* definition would be very useful. I would say the same about Cosmic Consciousness as Unamuno has said about religion—that it is better described than defined, and better felt than described. I think that one can get a true feeling for the phrase only by seeing it used in many contexts. Indeed, Bucke says about the above definition:

> What these words mean cannot be touched upon here; it is the business of this volume to throw some light upon them. There are many elements belonging to the Cosmic Sense besides the central fact just alluded to. Of these a few may be mentioned. Along with the consciousness of the cosmos there occurs an intellectual enlightenment or illumination which alone could place the individual on a new plane of existence—would make him almost a member of a new species. To this is added a state of moral exaltation, an indescribable feeling of elevation, elation and joyousness, and a quickening of the moral sense, which is fully as striking and more important to the individual and to the race than is the enhanced intellectual power. With these come, what might be called a sense of immortality, a consciousness of eternal life, not a conviction that he shall have this, but the consciousness that he has it already. (p. 3)

I believe the above paragraph should give the reader some feeling for Cosmic Consciousness.

Elsewhere, Bucke says:

> There is presented to his consciousness a clear conception (a vision) in outline of the meaning and drift of the universe. He does not come to believe, merely; but he sees and knows that the cosmos, which to the self conscious mind seems made up of dead matter, is in fact far otherwise—is in truth a living presence. He sees that instead of men being, as it were, patches of life scattered through an infinite sea of non-living substance, they are in reality specks of relative death in an infinite ocean of life. He sees that the life which is in man is eternal, as all life is eternal; that the soul of man is as immortal as God is; that the

universe is so built and ordered that without any paradventure all things work together for the good of each and all; that the foundation principle of the world is what we call love, and that the happiness of every individual is in the long run absolutely certain. The person who passes through this experience will learn in the few minutes, or even moments, of its continuance more than in months or years of study, and he will learn much that no study ever taught or can teach. (p. 73)

Here Bucke has used the word "God," which he rarely uses. I am not sure whether he thinks of Cosmic Consciousness as the direct awareness of a *personal* God, or of a more pantheistic deity, or whether this is left open. The second alternative seems the most likely, since elsewhere he says that Cosmic Consciousness shows that the universe is God and that God is the universe.

The author says further:

> Only a personal experience of it, or a prolonged study of men who have passed into the new life, will enable us to realize what this actually is. . . .
>
> It is impossible for the merely self-conscious man to form any conception of what this oncoming of Cosmic Consciousness must be to those who experience it. The man is lifted out of his old self and lives rather in heaven upon the old earth—more correctly the old earth becomes heaven. (p. 3)

This sounds a good deal like the Christian expression of conversion, doesn't it? Except that the oncoming of Cosmic Consciousness doesn't necessarily involve any change of religious *belief!* I'll say more about this when I come to discussing Havelock Ellis.

Another very important aspect of Cosmic Consciousness is the loss of the sense of *sin*; yet, this goes hand in hand with an elevation of the moral sense—a most noteworthy combination! Also, a frequent symptom of the Cosmic Conscious state is an increased attractiveness of the personality—a sort of charisma.

Next comes a very significant idea:

> The trait that distinguishes these people from other men is this: Their spiritual eyes have been opened and they have seen. The better known members of this group who, were they collected together, could be accommodated all at one time in a modern drawing-room, have created all the great modern religions, beginning with Taoism and Buddhism, and speaking generally, have created through religion and literature, modern civilization. Not that they have contributed any large numer-

ical proportion of the books that have been written, but that they have produced the few books which have inspired the larger number of all that have been written in modern times. These men dominate the last twenty-five, especially the last five, centuries as stars of the first magnitude dominate the midnight sky. (p. 11)

Thus Bucke, like Carpenter, believes that Cosmic Consciousness is the real source of all the world's religions. Now, he did not believe that the Cosmic Sense is necessarily infallible. Like the development of any faculty, it takes a long time to become perfected. And so just because Cosmic Consciousness is the *root* of religious beliefs, doesn't mean that the beliefs are necessarily correct!

Bucke has a prophetic vision of the future when Cosmic Consciousness comes to the entire human race. All religions known today will be melted down, and there will be no more priests, churches, creeds, revelations. Intermediaries of any kind will no longer be necessary, since people will then *directly* perceive what religious or mystical truth there is. This is another very important aspect of Cosmic Consciousness—it is completely nonauthoritarian. Or, rather, the Cosmic Sense is not dependent on any *belief* in authority; it carries its own authority.

So much for Cosmic Consciousness in general. The bulk of Bucke's book is devoted to an analysis of the writings of fifty selected persons whom the author believes to have had Cosmic Consciousness—fourteen who have had it totally and the others partially. The first group comprises Buddha, Jesus, St. Paul, Plotinus, Mohammed, Dante, Bartalomé de Las Casas, St. John of the Cross, William Shakespeare, Jacob Boehme, William Blake, Honoré de Balzac, Walt Whitman, and Edward Carpenter. Among the cases of *partial* Cosmic Consciousness, the author includes Moses, Gideon, Isaiah, Lao-tzu, Socrates, Roger Bacon, Blaise Pascal, Benedict de Spinoza, Emanuel Swedenborg, William Wordsworth, Aleksandr Pushkin, Ralph Waldo Emerson, Alfred Lord Tennyson, Henry David Thoreau, Ramakrishna, Richard Jeffries, and Horace Traubel.

Even if there is no metaphysical significance to Bucke's idea, even if his magnificently prophetic vision is only a beautiful pipe dream, his book should be of great value to even the most skeptical readers, because the analysis and comparison of the writings of these fifty individuals are of enormous psychological, philosophical, aesthetic, and literary interest. (For example, his analysis of some of the Shakespeare sonnets puts them in a very different light! Likewise, his analysis of some of the religious writings.) The reader will certainly *sense* something in common with all these writings, though he may not be able to define what it is, and what it really is might aptly be called *Cosmic Consciousness.*

Of course, the author's choice of subjects was largely subjective. Many known writers could surely be added to the list, and there are probably countless cases of Cosmic Consciousness of people who are totally unknown. I take a somewhat different attitude toward Cosmic Consciousness than does Bucke—I believe that Cosmic Consciousness is a matter of degree, just as everyone has *some* musical sense and *some* sense of humor. In some, it may exist in such a faint degree as to be barely on the threshold of recognizability. Others may have it to a degree a bit above this, but out of skepticism may repress the knowledge that they have it. I also think that Bucke's division of cases into total and partial is quite subjective— for example, why did he rank Buddha as total and Lao-tzu as partial? I would have tended toward the opposite!

The author believes, incidentally, that the intensity of Cosmic Consciousness grows through the centuries and that the most complete case known to date is that of Walt Whitman, whom Dr. Bucke knew personally and attended as a physician. Whitman believed that Bucke saved his life. He also said, "Someone was here the other day and complained that the Doctor was extreme. The sun's extreme too, and ain't I extreme?" Again: "It's beautiful to watch him at his work—to see how he can handle difficult people with such an easy manner"; and "Bucke is a man who enjoys being busy . . . is swift of execution, lucid, sure, decisive."

I find it amusing that when Bucke told Whitman that he had Cosmic Consciousness, Whitman seemed quite unimpressed, shrugged his shoulders in a good-natured way, as if to say, "If it makes you happy to think of it that way, by all means do so!" As Bucke says in his chapter on Whitman, "Walt Whitman, in my talks with him at that time, always disclaimed any lofty intention in himself or his poems. If you accepted his explanations they were simple and commonplace. But when you came to think about these explanations, and to enter into the spirit of them, you found that the simple and commonplace with him included the ideal and the spiritual" (p. 218).

The whole chapter on Whitman is superb! Here is another choice part: "I never knew him to be in a bad temper. He seemed to be always pleased with those about him. . . . People could not tell why they liked him. They said there was something attractive about him; that he had a great deal of personal magnetism, or made some other vague explanation that meant nothing" (p. 219). Incidentally, many people—particularly psychiatrists—are quite suspicious of those who never lose their temper: they claim that such people are not really free from anger, but are only suppressing or, more likely, repressing it. Even Bucke says that for a long time he was amazed at how well Whitman controlled his temper until he finally realized that Whitman simply didn't have any temper to control! In his own words:

> When I first knew Walt Whitman I used to think that he watched himself, and did not allow his tongue to give expression to feelings of fretfulness, antipathy, complaint and remonstrance.
> It did not occur to me as possible that these mental states could be absent in him. After long observation, however, and talking to others who had known him for many years, I satisfied myself that such absence or unconsciousness was entirely real. (p. 223)

I know that many psychiatrists will totally disapprove of this— indeed, I once asked a psychiatrist who was then a friend of mine whether one cannot learn to live without anger. He replied, "I wouldn't want to." When I asked him why, he replied, "Because I *enjoy* expressing my anger! Life without anger would be too bland." I must say, that reply amazed me! When I think of the vast number of exhilarating experiences in life that do not involve anger, I am flabbergasted that one should believe that life without anger is necessarily *bland!* I reported this conversation to another friend of mine who is an excellent mathematician and a Buddhist. He said, "Oh, yes; I can understand that. I don't agree with it, but I understand it. Some people simply need a high level of emotional intensity to keep going." Well, I am still puzzled: Why is anger necessary for a high emotional intensity?

My former friend the psychiatrist, by the way, calls himself an orthodox Freudian, and I am reminded that Freud considered a hated enemy indispensable to his emotional health. By contrast, I cannot help but think of Havelock Ellis (who was a good friend of Freud), who wrote, "Why indeed should one ever be hostile? What a vain thing is this hostility!" (Ellis 1923b, p. 123). A particularly revealing incident about Ellis occurred in his boyhood. One day he came home with a prominent hole (which was made with a pencil by one of his schoolmates) in the back of his neck. His mother indignantly said, "I hope you paid him back." To which Ellis replied, "No, for then I should have been as bad as he was."

Havelock Ellis is perhaps best known as a sexologist, which is unfortunate, since he has written so profusely and insightfully on such a large variety of subjects—psychology, philosophy, religion, mysticism, literature, travels, life in general, etc. At the age of nineteen, he had a "conversion" which I find of particular interest, for reasons I will shortly state. Now, the whole subject of conversion is of intense interest to me (I have avidly read James's *Varieties of Religious Experience* several times), and what is so remarkable and intriguing about the conversion of Ellis is that it involved no change of religious beliefs—only a profound change of attitude! Indeed, he had lost his boyhood religious ideas *before* his conversion.

In childhood he was brought up far from the conventional religious atmosphere and received little religious instruction outside his home, but felt from his earliest years that religion is a very personal matter. He accepted the creed set before him and studied the New Testament for his own satisfaction. This was till the age of twelve. Then came a period of critical and scientific investigation, with the realization that there were other religious beliefs that were incompatible or even inconsistent with Christianity. Then a process of disintegration took place in slow stages that were not realized until the process was complete: He at last realized that he no longer possessed any religious faith. This was at the age of seventeen. Hardly any changes of conduct resulted; the revolution was so gradual and natural that there was virtually no inward shock.

At the age of nineteen came what Ellis refers to as his *conversion*—his whole attitude toward the universe changed from hostility and dread to confidence and love. And for the first time, he then knew exactly the plan of his life which he indeed carried out. In his own words:

> The effect of that swift revolution was permanent. At first there was a moment or two of wavering, and then the primary exaltation subsided into an attitude of calm serenity towards all those questions that had once seemed so torturing. In regard to all these matters I had become permanently satisfied and at rest, yet absolutely unfettered and free. I was not troubled about the origin of the "soul" or about its destiny; I was entirely prepared to accept any analysis of the "soul"

which might command itself as reasonable. Neither was I troubled about the existence of a superior being or beings, and I was ready to see that all the words and forms by which men try to picture spiritual realities are mere metaphors and images of an inward experience. There was not a single clause in my religious creed because I held no creed. I had found that dogmas were—not, as I had once imagined, true, not, as I had afterwards supposed, false—but the mere shadows of intimate personal experience. I had become indifferent to shadows for I held the substance. (Ellis 1923a, p. 217)

That last sentence reminds me of a line of Whitman's: "I send no agent or medium, offer no representative of value, but offer the value itself" (Whitman 1885, p. 146).

Now, the conservative orthodox religionist would hardly regard Ellis's experience described above as a "conversion," since there is no move toward or away from a personal God. But it certainly qualifies as a conversion to the psychologist of religion because of the drastic psychological readjustment involved. Elsewhere, Ellis cannot help using the physical analogy of a dislocated jaw: "The miserable man is out of harmony with himself and the universe. But a surgeon comes along, and applying a little pressure at the right places, the jaw springs into place and the man's harmony is restored" (Ellis 1923a, p. 219). As Ellis says, this is but a crude and imperfect analogy which may help some minds to have an idea of what the conversion experience is like. More generally, the change is fundamentally a

readjustment of psychic elements to each other, enabling the whole machine to work harmoniously. There is no necessary introduction of new ideas; there is much more likely to be a casting out of dead ideas which have clogged the vital process. The psychic organism—which in conventional religion is called the "soul"—had not been in harmony with itself; now it is revolving truly on its own axis, and in doing so it simultaneously finds its true orbit in the cosmic system. In becoming one with itself, it becomes one with the universe. (pp. 218–19)

Now, this really sounds to me very much like a case of Cosmic Consciousness! Why did Bucke never write about him? Didn't he know about Ellis, or if he did, did he see matters differently? Ellis has another interesting thing to say about conversion:

People who come in contact with the phenomenon of "conversion" are obsessed by the notion that it must have something to do with morality. They seem to fancy that it is something that happens to a person leading a bad life whereby he suddenly leads a good life. That is a delusion. Whatever virtue morality may possess, it is outside the mystic's sphere. No doubt a person who has been initiated into this mystery is likely to be moral because he is henceforth in harmony with himself, and such a man is usually, by a natural impulse, in harmony also with others. (p. 223)

What a lovely attitude Ellis shows toward morality! I have often enjoyed asking people (particularly ministers) the following question: "Do you think of altruism as sacrificing one's happiness for the sake of others', or as gaining one's happiness through others?" (The usual response is "I've never thought about that before.") Kant, of course, would have preferred the former as having more "moral" worth. Ellis, I would say, would prefer the latter. I am also reminded of what Walt Whitman says about *duties:*

> I give nothing as duties,
> What others give as duties, I give as living impulses. (Whitman 1885,
>   p. 225)

This is about the antithesis of Kantian ethics! What Kant believes should be done out of "obedience to moral law," Whitman does out of simple human kindness, love, and sympathy. (For example, his service to wounded soldiers during the Civil War. I think Whitman would have been quite puzzled had he been told that he was doing this out of "duty.")

Ellis, by the way, was a great admirer of Walt Whitman. In a letter to his friend Olive Schreiner, he wrote, "His Leaves of Grass reveals, I think, the greatest heart now on earth. . . . Whitman is outside us—beyond and above us, and reveals what we should never have known if he hadn't told us" (quoted in Peterson 1928, p. 125). I strongly recommend the fascinating biography of Ellis by Houston Peterson and, of course, Ellis's *The Dance of Life.* The latter contains a chapter, "The Art of Religion," which is excellent, and I think it would be well if more people were familiar with the following passage:

> If at some period in the course of civilization we seriously find that our science and religion are antagonistic, then there must be something wrong with both. For if the natural impulses which normally work best together are separated and specialized in different persons, we may expect to find a concomitant state of atrophy and hypertro-

phy, both alike morbid. The scientific person will become atrophied on the mystical side, the mystical person will become atrophied on the scientific side. Each will become morbidly hypertrophied on his own side. But the assumption that, because there is a lack of harmony between opposing pathological states, there must also be a similar lack of harmony in the normal state, is unreasonable. We must seriously put out of court alike the hypertrophied scientific people with atrophied religious instincts, and the hypertrophied religious people with atrophied scientific instincts. Neither group can help us here; they only introduce confusion. . . .

The difficulty is not diminished when the person who is thus hypertrophied on one side and atrophied on the other suddenly wakes up to his one-sided state and hastily attempts to remedy it. The very fact that such a one-sided development has come about indicates that there has probably been a congenital basis for it, an innate disharmony which must require infinite patience and special personal experience to overcome. (Ellis 1923a, pp. 197, 199)

I question whether what Ellis calls "congenital" is really entirely so—it may well be environmental also. But this is a minor point. I particularly appreciated what Ellis said about one-sidedness. I also wonder whether that which he calls "religious instincts" is ultimately the same thing as that which Bucke calls "Cosmic Consciousness." And so we are back to Bucke's book and in particular to Walt Whitman.

First, let me tell you that in a charming poem, "Solitary Pleasures," the Japanese author Tachibama Akemi describes various pleasures of life, and in one of his verses he says:

> It is a pleasure
> When, in a book which by chance
> I am perusing
> I come on a character
> Who is exactly like me. (Keene 1935, pp. 174–75)

Well, I also like to come across characters just like me, and I so I was delighted to come across the following observation by Bucke about the reading habits of Walt Whitman:

Though he would sometimes not touch a book for a week, he generally spent a part (though not a large part) of each day in reading. Perhaps he would read on an average a couple of hours a day. He seldom read any book deliberately through, and there was no more (apparent) system about his reading than in anything else that he did; that is to say, there was no system about it at all. If he sat in the library an hour, he would have half a dozen volumes about him, on the table, on chairs and on the floor. He seemed to read a few pages here and a few pages there, and pass from place to place, from volume to volume, doubtless pursuing some clue or thread of his own. Sometimes (though very seldom) he would get sufficiently interested in a volume to read it all. (Bucke 1956, p. 219)

I cannot help recall a lady I know—a very conventional English teacher—who insists that in reading a book one should always read it from cover to cover without skipping a word! How silly can one get? This procedure is certainly appropriate in *some* situations, but in others, Whitman's sporadic methods are precisely what is called for.

As I have said, Bucke's whole chapter is excellent. This, and the chapter on Edward Carpenter, of which I will speak later, may well be the two best chapters of the book.

There is one passage of Whitman, which Bucke did not mention, that I have found particularly intriguing and impressive:

> There is something comes home to one now and perpetually,
> It is not what is printed, preached, discussed—it eludes discussion
> and print,
> It is not to be put in a book—it is not in this book,
> It is for you, whoever you are—it is no farther from you than your
> hearing and sight are from you,
> It is hinted by nearest, commonest, readiest—it is not them, though
> it is endlessly provoked by them, (what is there ready and near
> you now?)
>
> You may read in many languages, yet read nothing about it,
> You may read the President's Message, and read nothing about it
> there,
> Nothing in the reports from the State department or Treasury
> department, or in the daily papers or the weekly papers,
> Or in the census returns, assessors' returns, prices current, or any
> accounts of stock. (Whitman 1885, p. 44)

One thing that impresses me about this passage is that it suggests the very opposite of what is asserts—namely, it gives the feeling that it (Cosmic Consciousness?) *is* in the President's Message, reports of the State and Treasury departments, census reports, assessors' returns, and accounts of stock! It suggests that mysticism and everyday life are ultimately one and the same thing.

I am particularly interested in some of the things Whitman has to say concerning the relation of logic (a favorite subject of mine) to reality. What follows is a montage of various portions of *Leaves of Grass:*

> Swiftly arose and spread around me the peace and joy and knowledge that pass all the art and argument of the earth.
>
> A morning-glory at my window satisfies me more than the metaphysics of books.
>
> And a mouse is miracle enough to stagger sextillions of infidels.
>
> Logic and sermons never convince,
> The damp of the night drives deeper into my soul.
>
> When a university course convinces like a slumbering woman and child convince!
>
> To elaborate is no avail—learned and unlearned feel that it is so.
>
> Writing and talk do not prove me,
> I carry the plenum of proof, and everything else, in my face,
> With the hush of my lips I confound the topmost skeptic.
>
> I and mine do not convince by arguments, similes, rhymes,
> We convince by our presence.
>
> Let contradictions prevail! Let one thing contradict another! and let one line of my poems contradict another!
>
> The maker of poems settles justice, reality, immortality.
>
> Now I absorb immortality and peace,
> I admire death and test propositions
> Great is Wickedness—I find I often admire it, just as much as I admire goodness.
> Do you call that a paradox? It certainly is a paradox.
>
> The earth does not argue.
>
> No reasoning, no proof has established it,
> Undeniable growth has established it.
>
> The clock indicates the moment—but what does eternity indicate?
>
> Now I reëxamine philosophies and religions,
> They may prove well in lecture-rooms, yet not prove at all under the spacious clouds, and along the landscape and flowing currents.
>
> Here is the test of wisdom,
> Wisdom is not finally tested in schools,
> Wisdom cannot be passed from one having it, to another not having it.
> Wisdom is of the Soul, is not susceptible of proof, is its own proof.

Bucke has something interesting to say about Whitman's lack of sense of sin (which is one of the earmarks of Cosmic Consciousness): "This must not be understood as meaning that he felt himself to be perfect. Whitman realized his own greatness as clearly and fully as did any of his admirers. He also realized how immeasurably he was below the ideal which he constantly set up before himself" (Bucke 1956, p. 237).

It is with difficulty that I leave the chapter on Walt Whitman, but I must say a little on some of the other chapters. I didn't find the chapter on Buddha too interesting, and I got from it very little feel for Cosmic Consciousness. One little point of interest: Concerning Buddha's statement that the enlightened men are free in their hearts from the longing after a future life, Bucke says, "A man who has acquired the Cosmic Sense does not desire eternal life—he has it." I also found the chapter on Jesus quite disappointing—Bucke could really have chosen better sayings of Jesus to analyze. I got virtually no feeling of Cosmic Consciousness from this chapter.

The chapter on St. Paul I found vastly better! There I really got the feeling of Cosmic Consciousness to an extraordinary degree (much more, for some odd reason, than reading Paul in the New Testament). Of course, "Christ" for Bucke is but another name for Cosmic Consciousness:

> If any man is in Christ he is a new creature; the old things are passed away; behold they are become new. (II Corinthians 5:17)

About this Bucke says:

> No expression could be more clear cut, more perfect. The man who enters Cosmic Consciousness is really a new creature and all his surroundings "become new"—take on a new face and meaning. You get around to the other side of things, as it were; they are the same, but also entirely different. As said by Walt Whitman: "Things are not diminished from the places they hold before. The earth is just as positive and direct as it was before. But the soul is also real; it too is positive and direct; no reasoning, no proof has established it, undeniable growth has established it." (p. 119)

Another example:

> Christ redeemed us from the curse of the law. . . . But before faith came, we were kept inward under the law, shut up into faith which should afterwards be revealed. So that the law has been our tutor to bring us into Christ that we might be justified by faith; but now that

faith is come we are no longer under a tutor. For ye are all sons of God
through faith in Jesus Christ. For as many of you as were baptized
into Christ did put on Christ. (Galatians 3:13, 23–27)

Bucke has this observation:

> Christ is the Cosmic Sense conceived as a distinct entity or individu-
> ality. That *does* redeem any to whom it comes from the "cause of the
> law"—i.e. from the shame and fear and hate that belongs to the self
> conscious life. Paul seems to suppose a baptism *into* Cosmic Con-
> sciousness [Christ]. Doubtless there *is* such a baptism; but where is
> the priesthood which is able to administer it? (p. 116)

I myself would like to say the following about Paul's passage: To
me, one of the most attractive ideas in the whole Christian philosophy is Paul's idea that when one has attained a certain degree of
spirituality (which Paul calls "putting on Christ" and Bucke calls
"achieving Cosmic Consciousness"), one no longer needs moral
law. One of the things I love about the Chinese Taoists is that they
had the same idea (though phrased differently—phrased as "being
in harmony with the Tao"). Once, in a cynical mood, I defined *morality* as that which is needed by people who are deficient in goodness. Actually, this is not purely cynical but is essentially the Taoist
idea that the need for morality is indicative of being out of harmony with the Tao. Put more positively, one who is in harmony
with the Tao does the right thing, not because it is the "moral thing
to do," but because one feels like it. Or as Paul has said elsewhere,
the man in grace has an immediate *abhorrence* of sinning.

As I see it, there is something transcendental, for want of a better
term, I call *Spirituality*. And I heartily agree with some Christian
writers (e.g., Henry Drummond) who believe that the lowest stage
of spirituality is higher than the highest stage of morality, and that
the highest stage of morality is not even possible without some degree of spirituality. In my earlier writings, I have expressed very
negative attitudes toward morality. I now see the matter in a different and, I believe, a better light. As I now see it (partly through a
study of yoga philosophy), morality is appropriate to certain stages
of one's spiritual development, but after these stages are passed,
morality becomes no longer necessary. Isn't this essentially the
same thing that Paul said?

Next, the chapter on Plotinus: I very much enjoyed this chapter,
not particularly for the things Bucke said, but for the ideas of Ploti-

nus himself. Here is a portion of a letter from Plotinus to a friend named Flaccus:

> You ask, how can we know the Infinite? I answer, not by reason. It is the office of reason to distinguish and define. The Infinite, therefore, cannot be ranked among its objects. You can only apprehend the Infinite by a faculty superior to reason, by entering into a state in which you are your finite self no longer—in which the divine essence is communicated to you. . . . It is the liberation of your mind from its finite consciousness. Like only can apprehend like; when you thus cease to be finite, you become one with the Infinite. In the reduction of your soul to its simplest self, its divine essence, you realize this union—this identity.
>
> But this sublime condition is not of permanent duration. It is only now and then that we can enjoy this elevation. . . . I myself have realized it but three times as yet. . . . All that tends to purify and elevate the mind will assist in this attainment, and facilitate the approach and the recurrence of these happy intervals. There are, then, different roads by which this end may be reached. The love of beauty which exalts the poet; that devotion to the One and that ascent of science which makes the ambition of the philosopher and that love and those prayers by which some devout and ardent soul tends in its moral purity towards perfection. These are the great highways conducting to that height above the actual and the particular, where we stand in the immediate presence of the Infinite, who shines out as from the deeps of the soul. (quoted by Bucke, p. 121)

I must tell you of an incident. For several years I have been having a running controversy with a musician who is extremely suspicious of and antithetical to anything smacking of mysticism or religion. I recently read her the above passage of Plotinus's. To my agreeable surprise, she said, "That is excellently expressed—*excellently!* I wish I could feel that way, but I cannot!" That only confirmed what I had suspected all along—that her hostility to mysticism was caused by envy. I then said to her, "But don't you get this sometimes through your music?" She replied, "In a way, yes, but I cannot verbalize it like that." Well, good for her! Why verbalize?

In the next chapter on Mohammed, Bucke quotes the following from the Qur'an (trans. E. H. Palmer): "And listen for the day when the crier shall cry from a near place—the day when they shall hear the shout in truth—that is the day of coming forth." About this, Bucke says that the suddenness and unexpectedness of the oncoming of Cosmic Consciousness is noted in the writings of nearly all of those who have experienced illumination. He then quotes a passage of Edward Carpenter's from *Towards Democracy:*

> That day—the day of deliverance—shall come to you in what place you know not; it shall come, but you know not the time. In the pulpit while you are preaching the sermon, behold! Suddenly the ties and the bands shall drop off; in the prison One shall come and you shall go free forever. In the fields, with the plough and chain-harrow; by the side of your horse in the stall; in the midst of fashionable life; in making and receiving morning calls; in your drawing room—even there, who knows? It shall duly at the appointed hour come. (Carpenter 1892b, p. 231)

I really find it amazing that two such utterly different individuals as Mohammed and Edward Carpenter (a nineteenth-century socialist, adjudicator for women's rights, and nontheistic mystic) should have such similar ideas! One of the excellent things about Bucke's book is the unification of ideas of so many different thinkers!

In the chapter on Dante and his *Divine Comedy,* Bucke comments almost exclusively on passages from the *Paradiso,* and on none from the *Inferno.* But he does have something interesting to say about the following from the *Purgatorio* (trans. Charles Eliot Norton), which is said to Dante by Virgil:

> Expect no more or word or sign from me. Free, upright and sane in thine own free will, and it would be wrong not to act according to its pleasure; wherefore thee over thyself I crown and mitre. (Dante 1892, p. 176)

I would like to point out two other translations of this passage. The following is by Longfellow:

> Expect no more word or sign from me;
> Free and upright and sound is thy freedom
> And error were it not to do its bidding;
> Thee o'er thyself I therefore crown and mitre. (Dante 1909, p. 163)

This translation is quite similar, though I prefer in the last line the deletion of "therefore." The next translation by Lawrence Grant White is both more clear and less poetic:

> Expect no further speech or sign from me.
> Your will, upright and sound, is now released: You'll do no wrong, if you but do its bidding; Wherefore I crown you sovereign of yourself. (Dante 1948, p. 114)

About this passage (the Norton translation) Bucke says, "When the Cosmic Sense comes the rules and standards belonging to self consciousness are suspended. . . . No man with the Cosmic Sense will take direction (in the affairs of the soul) from any other man or from any so-called God. In his own heart he holds the highest accessible standard, and to that he will and must adhere; that only can he obey (Bucke 1956, p. 135). Bravo! It does indeed seem that the cases of Cosmic Consciousness cited by Bucke tend to be independent of authority—the authority of other people, that is; not the authority of Cosmic Consciousness, which is self-authenticating. Let us note carefully about people who have the Cosmic Sense: Bucke didn't say that they wouldn't take direction from God, but from any *so-called* God. Indeed, a person who refuses to obey those directives *said* to be from God may, in fact, be obeying God.

I will not be discussing all of Bucke's fourteen cases of Cosmic Consciousness, but only those I found of most interest. The next one I wish to discuss is that of Shakespeare. But first I must tell the reader of two ideas of Bucke that strike me as absolutely crazy, and that almost (but fortunately didn't) turn me away from the entire book! The first is that color vision is only of recent origin (even the ancient Greeks knew only three or four different colors), and the second is that it was really Francis Bacon who wrote the plays attributed to Shakespeare. I believe both these ideas are ridiculous and can only console myself by realizing that a person can be crazy in some areas and absolutely brilliant in others. After giving reasons why it was Bacon who wrote the plays, I am glad that Bucke then said, "But the present volume has nothing to do with the Bacon-Shakespeare question except incidentally, by the way, and perforce. *Somebody* wrote the plays and 'Sonnets,' and that person, whoever he might be, had, it is believed Cosmic Consciousness" (p. 167).

The interesting thing about this chapter is Bucke's commentary on twenty-two of the Shakespeare sonnets. Whereas most people believe that the sonnets were addressed to a lover (male or female), Bucke believes them to be addressed to the Cosmic Conscious sense. Whether the reader agrees with this or not, it certainly puts the sonnets in an unusual and interesting light! I will give one sample:

> Sin of self-love possesseth all mine eyes
> And all my soul, and all my every part;
> And for this sin there is no remedy,

It is so grounded inward in my heart.
Methinks no face so gracious is as mine,
No shape so true, no truth of such account;
And for myself my own worth do define,
As I all other in all worth surmount.
But when my glass shows me myself indeed,
Beaten and chopp'd with tann'd antiquity,
Mine own self-love quite contrary I read;
Self so self-loving were iniquity.
'Tis thee (myself) that for myself I praise,
Painting my age with beauty of thy days. (Sonnet 62)

Here is what Bucke says:

In this sonnet the duality of the person writing is brought out very strongly—no doubt purposely. When he dwells on his Cosmic Conscious self he is, as it were, lost in admiration of himself. When he turns to the physical and self-conscious he is inclined, on the contrary, to despise himself. He is at the same time very much and very little of an egotist. Those who knew the man Walt Whitman know that this same seeming contradiction resting on the same foundation existed most markedly in him. Whitman's admiration for the Cosmic Conscious Whitman and his works (the "Leaves") was just such as was pictured in this sonnet, while he was absolutely devoid of egotism in the ordinary way of the self conscious individual. It is believed that the above remarks would remain true if applied to Paul, Mohammed or Balzac. Reduced to last analysis, the matter seems to stand about as follows: The Cosmic Conscious self, from all points of view, appears superb, divine. From the point of view of the Cosmic Conscious self, the body and the self conscious self appear equally divine. But from the point of view of the ordinary self consciousness, and so compared with the Cosmic Conscious self, the self conscious self and the body seem insignificant and even, as well shown in Paul's case contemptible. (p. 174)

I wonder what Shakespeare in Heaven would think of this analysis? I can imagine his saying something like "Interesting idea! I never thought of my sonnet that way, but I guess his way is one of many interesting possible ways of looking at it."

My point, of course, is that Bucke's analysis is interesting irrespective of whether or not Shakespeare really had this in mind. At any rate, the sonnet *inspired* Bucke with the interesting idea that the Superior Self respects both the Superior Self and the Inferior Self, whereas the latter respects only the former. It is quite possible that Bucke would never have thought of this had he not read the sonnet.

I wish to interject a personal remark: I have always had great difficulty in understanding the *meaning* of Shakespeare's sonnets, yet I find the *sound* of them so beautiful! Shakespeare must have had an extremely musical ear.

Coming back to Bucke, many of his commentaries are not so much analyses as thought inspired by the material. He, as it were, reads a passage and takes off from there! The chapter on William Blake is very interesting. Bucke quotes the following from a memoir by W. M. Rossetti:

> As to his religious belief, it should be understood that Blake was a Christian in a certain way, and a truly fervent Christian; but it was a way of his own, exceedingly different from any of the churches. For the last forty years of his life he never entered a place of worship.
>
> He believed—with a great profundity and ardor of faith—in God; but believed also that men are gods, or that collective man is God. He believed in Christ; but exactly what he believed him to be is a separate question. "Jesus Christ," he said, conversing with Mr. Robinson, "is the only God, and so am I, and so are you." (p. 195)

I cannot help but recall a cute incident of a lovely lady I know who once said to one of her two dogs, "You're my favorite dog!" She then turned to the other and said, "You're also my favorite dog!"

To continue with the passage on Blake:

> In immortality Blake seems to have believed implicitly, and (in some main essentials) without much deviation from other people's credence. When he heard of Flaxman's death (December 7, 1826) he observes, "I cannot think of death as more than the going out of one room into another." In one of his writings he says: "The world of imagination is the world of eternity. It is the divine bosom into which we shall all go after the death of the vegetated body."

Here is what Bucke says:

> Blake's religion—his attitude toward the church—toward God—toward immortality—is the characteristic attitude of the man who has attained to Cosmic Consciousness—as shown in each life and in all the writings of these men.
>
> His attitude toward death is that of all the illuminati. He does not think he will be immortal. He *has* eternal life. (ibid.)

Now it is with pleasure that I turn to Edward Carpenter. Carpenter was a man of many parts—a one-time minister who never profoundly believed in the historical accuracy of the Bible and who thought he could widen the church from the inside, but soon found out that he couldn't, and hence had to make a complete break with the church. Next he was a successful worker in university education, followed by a deep study of social questions with a growing conviction that society was on a wrong basis and moving in the wrong direction. He was also an accomplished musician and wrote a book on the Beethoven piano sonatas. I would say that he is known about equally as a social reformer and a writer on Cosmic Consciousness, the two interests which were integrated in his book *On Democracy* (Carpenter 1892b), which is a sort of counterpart to Whitman's *Leaves of Grass* and is generally considered to be his most important expression of Cosmic Consciousness. Personally, I get much more the feeling of Carpenter, the social reformer, from this book! Of course he, like Bucke, thinks of socialism and Cosmic Consciousness as coming hand in hand. Still, I get much more the feeling of the former than the latter from *On Democracy*. People to whom I have read the following verse have been most impressed:

O DEMOCRACY, I SHOUT FOR YOU!

Back! Make me a space round me, you kid-gloved rotten-breathed paralytic world, with miserable antics mimicking the appearance of life.

England! for good or evil it is useless to attempt to conceal yourself—I know you too well.

I am the very devil. I will tear your veils off, your false shows and pride I will trail in the dust—you shall be utterly naked before me, in your beauty and in your shame.

For who better than I should know your rottenness, your self-deceit, your delusion, your hideous grinning corpse—chattering death-in-life business on top? (and who better than I the wonderful hidden sources of your strength beneath?)

Deceive yourself no longer.

Do you think your smoothfaced Respectability will save you? or that Cowardice carries a master-key of the universe in its pocket—scrambling miserably out of the ditch on the hands of those beneath it?

Do you think that it is a fine thing to grind cheap goods out of the hard labor of ill-paid boys? and do you imagine that all your

Commerce Shows and Manufactures are anything at all compared
with the bodies and souls of these?

Do you suppose I have not heard your talk about Morality and
Religion and set it face to face in my soul to the instinct of one clean
naked unashamed Man? or that I have not seen your coteries of ele-
gant and learned people put to rout by the innocent speech of a
child, and the apparition of a mother suckling her own babe!

Do you think there ever was Infidelity greater than this?

Do you grab interest on Money and lose all interest in Life? Do
you found a huge system of national Credit on absolute personal
Distrust? Do you batten like a ghoul on the dead corpses of animals,
and then expect to be of a cheerful disposition? Do you put the
loving beasts to torture as a means of promoting your own health
and happiness? Do you, O foolishest one, fancy to bind men
together by Laws (of all ideas the most laughable), and set whole
tribes of unbelievers to work year after year patching that rotten net?
Do you live continually farther and farther from Nature, till you
actually doubt if there be any natural life, or any avenging instinct in
the dumb elements?—And then do you wonder that your own Life
is slowly ebbing—that you have lost all gladness and faith?

I do not a bit. I am disgusted with you, and will not cease till I
have absolutely floored you. I do not care; you may struggle; but I
am stronger. (Carpenter 1892b, pp. 20–22)

This poem criticizes not only economic evils, but also animal vivi-
section and the violation of nature (not realizing the "avenging instincts in the dumb elements"), which is so painfully pertinent to
our present-day pollution problems!

So much for Carpenter, the social reformer; we now turn to him
in relation to Cosmic Consciousness. I believe the phrase "Cosmic
Consciousness" is due to Carpenter, not to Bucke. Unlike Whitman, who never thought in terms of Cosmic Consciousness (even
though he achieved it), Carpenter *did* think in these terms and was
fully aware that he was in that state, which for want of better words
he called Cosmic Consciousness. When Bucke wrote him a letter
asking him to describe the state, Carpenter gave the following
modest reply:

I really do not feel that I can tell you anything without falsifying and
obscuring the matter. I have done my best to write it out in "Towards
Democracy." I have no experience of physical light in this relation.
The perception seems to be one in which all the senses unite into one
sense. In which *you become* the object. But this is unintelligible, men-

tally speaking. I do not think the matter can be defined as yet; but I do not know that there is any harm in writing about it. (Bucke 1956, p. 240)

In his book *Civilization: Its Cause and Cure,* Carpenter gives the following description:

> There is in every man a local consciousness connected with his quite external body; that we know. Are there not also in every man the making of a universal consciousness? That there are in us phases of consciousness which transcend the limit of the bodily senses is a matter of daily experience; that we perceive and know things which are not conveyed to us by our bodily eyes and heard by our bodily ears is certain; that rise in us waves of consciousness from those around us—from the people, the race to which we belong—is also certain. May these, then, not be in us the makings of a perception and knowledge which shall not be relative to this body which is here and now, but which shall be good for all time and everywhere? Does there not exist, in truth, as we have already hinted, an inner illumination, of which what we call light in the outer world is the partial expression and manifestation, by which we can ultimately see things *as they are?* (Carpenter 1889, p. 252)

Elsewhere (in *The Labor Prophet,* May 1894), Carpenter says, "There seems to be a vision possible to man, as from some more universal standpoint, free from the obscurity and localism which specially connect themselves with the passing clouds of desire, fear and all other ordinary thought and emotion" (quoted by Bucke).

Perhaps his most useful passages are from his book *From Adam's Peak to Elephanta;* his chapter "Consciousness Without Thought" was written as an idea of what Cosmic Consciousness is:

> The question is: What is this experience? or rather—since an experience can really only be known to a person who experiences it—we may ask: What is the nature of this experience? And in trying to indicate an answer of some kind to this question I feel considerable diffidence, just for the very reason (for one) already mentioned—namely, that it is so difficult or impossible for one person to give a true account of an experience which has occurred to another. (1892a, 153)

A bit later comes something quite important:

> If there is a higher form of consciousness obtainable by man than that which he can for the most part claim at present, it is probable—nay

certain—that it is evolving and will evolve but slowly and with many a skip and hesitant pause by the way. (p. 153)

Perfect! This fits in exactly with the idea that all of the world's religions, despite their errors, are all moving slowly but surely to the truth! And yet a bit farther on come the following sublime words:

> It is more than probable that in the hidden depths of time there lurks a consciousness which is not the consciousness of sensation and which is not the consciousness of self—or at least which includes and surpasses these—a consciousness in which the contrast between the ego and the external world, and the distinction between subject and object fall away. The part of the world into which such a consciousness admits us (call it supermundane or whatever you will) is probably at least as vast and complex as the part we know, and progress in that region at least equally slow and tentative and various, laborious, discontinuous and uncertain. There is no sudden leap out of the back parlor onto Olympus; and the routes, when found, from one to the other, are long and bewildering in their variety. (ibid.)

The writer Honoré de Balzac, on whom Bucke has a chapter, is perhaps not generally thought of as a mystic, but some of his ideas are closely related to what we have been discussing. Balzac's two most overtly mystical works are *Seraphita* and *Louis Lambert*—the latter is believed by many to be autobiographical. Curiously enough, Balzac uses the word "specialist" for a mystic, or one in the Cosmic Conscious state. He claimed that Jesus is a specialist and likewise Dante. The following is from *Louis Lambert:*

> The specialist is necessarily the loftiest expression of *man*—the link which connects the visible to the superior worlds. He acts, he sees, he feels through his *inner being*. The abstractive thinks. The instinctive simply acts.
> Hence three degrees for man. As an instinctive he is below the level; as an abstractive he attains to it; as a specialist he rises above it. Specialism opens to man his true career; the Infinite dawns upon him—he catches a glimpse of his destiny. (quoted by Bucke, p. 213)

With regard to the first paragraph, Bucke says:

> The state of Cosmic Consciousness is undoubtedly the highest that we can at present conceive, but it does not follow that there are no higher nor that we may not eventually attain to higher.

XV

Society begins in the sphere of Abstraction. If Abstraction [Intellectualization], as compared with instinct, is almost divine power, it is nevertheless incredibly weak as compared with the gift of Specialism, which is the formula of God. . . . From Abstraction are derived laws, arts, social ideals and interests. It is the glory and scourge of the earth; its glory because it has created social life; its scourge because it allows man to evade entering into Specialism, which is one of the paths to the Infinite. Man measures everything by Abstractions; Good and Evil, Virtue and Crime. . . . There must be intermediate beings, then, dividing the sphere of instinct from the sphere of Abstractions, to whom the two elements mingle in a infinite variety of proportions.

XVI

Specialism consists in seeing the things of the material universe and the things of the spiritual universe in all their ramifications, original and causative. The greatest human geniuses are those who started from the darkness of Abstraction to attain to the light of Specialism. (Specialism, *species*, sight; speculation, or seeing everything, and all at once; *Speculum*, a mirror or means of apprehending a thing by seeing the whole of it.) Jesus had the gift of Specialism; he saw each fact in the root and its results, in the past where it had its rise, and in the future where it would grow out and spread; His sight pierced into the understandings of others. The perfection of the inner eye gives rise to the gift of Specialism. Specialism brings with it Intuition. Intuition is one of the faculties of the Inner Man, of which Specialism is an attribute. Intuition acts by an imperceptible sensation of which he who obeys it is not conscious; for instance, Napoleon instinctively moving from a spot struck immediately afterwards by a cannon ball.

XVII

Between the sphere of Abstraction and that of Specialism, as between those of Abstraction and instinct, there are beings in whom the attributes of both combine and produce a mixture, these are the men of genius. (pp. 212–13)

Bertrand Russell says essentially the same thing in his famous essay "Mysticism and Logic":

Metaphysics, or the attempt to conceive the world as a whole by means of thought, has been developed, from the first, by the union and conflict of two very different impulses, the one urging men towards mysticism, the other urging them towards science. Some men have achieved greatness through one of those impulses alone, others through the other alone: in Hume, for example, the scientific impulse reigns quite unchecked, while in Blake a strong hostility to science co-exists with profound mystic insight. But the greatest men who have been philosophers have felt the need both of science and of mysticism; the attempt to harmonize the two was what made their life, and what always must, for all its arduous uncertainty, make philosophy, to some minds, a greater thing than either science or religion. (Russell 1929, p. 1)

Later in the essay, Russell says the following about reason and intuition:

The opposition of instinct and reason, is mainly illusory. Instinct, intuition, or insight is what first leads to the beliefs which subsequent reason confirms or confutes; but the confirmation, where it is possible, consists, in the last analysis, of agreement with other beliefs no less instructive. Reason is a harmonizing, controlling force rather than a creative one. Even in the most purely logical realm, it is insight that first arrives at what is new.

Incidentally, Russell's essay "A Free Man's Worship" (found in the same volume) really took me by surprise! It is one of the best religious pieces I have ever read—and in a way I am not too happy with it; it is a little *too* humble! (I believe in a healthy balance between humility and pride.) Anyway, had I not known that the author was Bertrand Russell, I would have judged it to have been written by the most devout Christian imaginable!

Continuing with Balzac:

XVIII

Specializing is necessarily the most perfect expression of man, and he is the link binding the visible world to the higher worlds; he acts, sees and feels by his inner powers. The man of abstraction thinks. The man of instinct acts.

XIX

Hence man has three degrees. That of Instinct, below the average; that of Abstraction, the general average; that of Specialism, above the average. Specialism opens to man his true career; the Infinite dawns on him; he sees what his destiny must be. (Bucke 1956, p. 213)

Bucke gives only three cases of Cosmic Consciousness among women, and these only partial. (He claims that the phenomenon is more frequent among males.) I cannot tell you the names of these three, since only their initials are given. He also mentions a fourth and very strong case, but regretfully cannot state it, as the female in question did not want her case to be made public—even anonymously.

I wonder if Bucke was familiar with George Sand's autobiographical account of her adolescent convent days and her conversion experience; it sounds to me very much like some of his accounts! As background, let me tell you that shortly after Sand's entry into the convent, she joined a mischievous group of girls who called themselves *les diables*. Then, some time later, something happened. In her own words:

> There came all at once, however, a great change in my life; and a passionate devotion blazed up spontaneously in a soul ignorant of itself. I was weary of idleness, of yielding to the caprices of my companions or following their lead,—tired, in short, of our long-continued, systematic rebellion against discipline . . . I was fifteen years old, with a great yearning for love, and a void in my heart. . . . I did not turn to God; but what Christians call divine grace came down to me, and took possession of me as if by surprise. (Sand 1893, p. 122)

What now comes is her conversion experience. In reading this, let us bear in mind that, according to Bucke, the onset of Cosmic Consciousness is almost invariably accompanied by the experience of being suddenly enveloped in a blinding light. The experience occurred in the evening in church, where she was not supposed to be at that time, but she had sneaked in:

> Enraptured with the poetry of the place, I lingered long after the nun had finished reading and had gone away. It was growing late; prayers were over, and it was time to close the church. I had lost all sense of time. I do not know exactly how it was, but it seemed as if I were breathing an atmosphere of indescribable sweetness, inhaling it more with my soul than with my senses. All at once I felt something like a shock and grew dizzy. A white light flashed before my eyes, in which I gradually seemed enveloped. . . .
>
> Knowing well that I was under a sort of hallucination, I was neither elated nor terrified. I did not say to myself that it was a miracle, or even a vainglorious deception, but I tried to see things as they really were; only I felt sure that faith had taken possession of my heart—as I had always hoped it might—and my face was bathed in tears of happiness and gratitude. . . . I felt all at once . . . as if an unsurmountable barrier had suddenly given way between the sources of infinite life

and the slumbering forces of my soul. I saw a long vista stretch out endlessly before me, and I longed to tread that road. There was no more doubt or lukewarmness, and it never occurred to me that I could regret or ridicule this passionate excitement; for I was one of those who never look behind. (p. 133)

I conjecture that if Bucke had known about this case, he would have included it—at least among the partial cases.

I was very curious that Sand said, "Knowing well that I was under a sort of hallucination. . . ." This speaks remarkably well for her objectivity, and this also brings me to another interesting point. According to Bucke, the onset of Cosmic Consciousness is often accompanied by the person having doubts of his own sanity:

> It seems that in every, or nearly every man who enters into cosmic consciousness apprehension is at first more or less excited, the person doubting whether the new sense may not be a symptom or form of insanity. Mohammed was greatly alarmed. I think it is clear that Paul was, and others to be mentioned further on were similarly affected.
>
> The first thing each person asks himself upon experiencing the new sense is: Does what I see and feel represent reality or am I suffering from a delusion? The fact that the new experience seems even more real than the old teachings of simple and self consciousness does not at first reassure him, because he probably knows that delusions, when present possess the mind just as firmly as do actual facts.
>
> True or not true, each person who has the experience in question eventually, perforce, believes in its teachings, accepting them as absolutely as any teachings whatsoever. This, however, would not prove them true, since the same might be said of the delusions of the insane. (Bucke 1956, p. 70)

Bucke then considers the question of how we shall know that this is a new sense, revealing fact, and not a form of insanity, plunging its subject into delusion? Frankly, I do not see the necessity of this drastic dichotomy! Even if some of the beliefs of those entering Cosmic Consciousness are false, it doesn't follow that they necessarily indicate insanity! (I am reminded of a silly thing said by C. S. Lewis about Jesus—that either he was what he claimed to be— God—or he was a madman. I say "rubbish"!) At any rate, Bucke applies the pragmatic test "by their fruits shall ye know them" and reasons that while in all forms of insanity, self-restraint and inhibition are greatly reduced, sometimes even abolished (and here Bucke is certainly right!), in Cosmic Consciousness it is enormously increased. That is certainly a good argument for not attributing insanity to those entering the state, but it does not prove that the new sense reveals objective *facts*. (I myself, however, believe it does, mainly for purely subjective reasons—namely, that the testimony borne by those entering the state strikes a resonance within me.)

Many of the cases of partial Cosmic Consciousness cited by Bucke are very interesting—as interesting as some of the total cases. Of particular interest is the experience of Alfred Lord Tennyson, which I found one of the clearest and most convincing that I know. Tennyson wrote in a letter:

> A kind of waking trance—this for lack of a better word—I have frequently had, quite up from boyhood, when I have been quite alone . . . All at once, as it were out of the intensity of the consciousness of individuality, individuality itself seemed to dissolve and fade away into boundless being, and this was not a confused state but the clearest, the surest of the sure, utterly beyond words—where death was an almost laughable impossibility—the loss of personality (if so it were) seeming no extinction but the only true life. (Tennyson 1897, p. 320)

I would like to compare this with the following passage from the Mandukya Upanishad. Its author has been discussing three normal kinds of mental condition, waking consciousness, dreaming, and dreamless sleep and then proceeds:

> The Fourth, say the wise . . . is not the knowledge of the senses, nor is it relative knowledge, nor yet inferential knowledge. Beyond the senses, beyond the understanding, beyond all expression, is the Fourth. It is pure unitary consciousness wherein awareness of the world and of multiplicity is completely obliterated. It is ineffable peace. It is the supreme Good. It is One without a second. It is the Self. (*Upanishads*, p. 51)

I wonder whether this "Fourth" kind of consciousness is the same as that which Bucke and Carpenter call Cosmic Consciousness. There are obvious similarities, yet these seem to be also some differences. For one thing, the Indian mystics stress the mystical vision that "All is One," which I cannot find very much in the accounts in Bucke.

Let us now look at Cosmic Consciousness in relation to Transcendentalism. In the book *On Cosmic Relations* the author, Henry Holt, says the following, which sounds to me very much like a cross between Transcendentalism and Cosmic Consciousness:

Indications are of a consciousness aware of everything that is going on or has gone on, at least within the sphere of its activity, and which includes and reaches far outside of our activity and our knowledge. All individual consciousnesses seem to be, in some mysterious way, not only for themselves, but part of that universal consciousness; for we get from it not only wondrous dream-images of all kinds, but mysterious impressions from individual consciousnesses, other than our own, which with our own are part of it.

But though perhaps we flow back into this constantly increasing aggregate of mind—the Cosmic Soul—it seems much more obviously to flow into us, at times and in degrees that vary enormously, as we vary. Into the least sensitive or receptive it does not go perceptibly beyond the ordinary psychoses of daily life; into others it seems to penetrate in ways to which we hardly know how to assign limits. Will it not presumably, as evolution goes on, flow more and more into all of us?

It looks too as if these possibilities might be the supreme justification for the evolution of the universe. There may be justification enough in birds and flowers, in the play of lambs and children, in sex, in love, in the maternity around which so much of the world's worship has centered, in knowledge, in wisdom, even as they have been ordinarily understood; but a new significance, a new joy, a new glory over and beyond them all sometimes seems to have been lately promised by that as yet dim conception of the Cosmic Soul.

Is this "Cosmic Soul" the same as the *Over-soul* of Emerson?

About the soul itself, Emerson says the following in his essay *Immortality:*

All goes to show that the soul in man is not an organ, but animates and exercises all the organs; is not a function, like the power of memory, of calculation, of comparison, but uses these as hands and feet; is not a faculty, but a light; is not the intellect of the will; is the background of our being, in which they lie—an immensity not possessed and that cannot be possessed. . . . The action of the soul is oftener in that which is felt and left unsaid than that which is said in any conversation. . . . The soul is the perceiver and revealer of truth. We know truth when we see it, let skeptic and scoffer say what they choose. Foolish people ask you, when you have spoken what they do not wish to hear. "How do you know it is truth and not an error of your own?" We know truth, when we see it, from opinion, as we know when we are awake that we are awake.

A bit later Emerson says the following, which ties in perfectly with Bucke's ideas:

> We distinguish the announcements of the soul, its manifestations of its own nature, by the term *Revelation*. These are always attended by the emotion of the sublime. . . . A thrill passes through all men at the reception of a new truth, or at the performance of a great action, which comes out of the heart of nature. . . . Every moment when the individual feels himself invaded by it is memorable. By the necessity of our constitution certain enthusiasm attends the individual's consciousness. . . . The character and duration of this enthusiasm vary with the state of the individual. . . . A certain tendency to insanity has always attended the opening of the religious sense, as if they had been "blasted with excess of light."

The comparison of this with Bucke is extremely interesting. Bucke does not say that illumination carries with it a tendency to insanity, but a *doubting* of one's sanity. But he adds, "If what is here called Cosmic Consciousness is a form of insanity, we are confronted by the terrible fact (were it not an absurdity) that our civilization, including our highest religions, rests on delusion" (Bucke 1956, p. 70).

Well, many people *do* believe that our so-called "higher religions" rest on delusions. Freud thought of religion as a mass psychosis, but I think he was referring primarily to the orthodox religions involving a personal God who "rules" the universe. I also think that what really bothered Freud the most about religion was not that it has no rational, scientific basis, but its authoritarian nature. Freud was so authoritarian that he couldn't bear any other authority! I also have the strong feeling that, deep down, Freud was scared to death that there really is a God who would punish him for not believing in Him.

Speaking of the experience of those entering the Cosmic Conscious state, Overstreet says:

> We may, to be sure, brush these experiences aside as aberrations. William James, however, warns us that it will not do to pooh-pooh them entirely away. Average minds may do that, and, in fact, do do it, but not scientific minds, to whom the extraordinary is simply an invitation to investigate and try to understand. But there is a particular reason why we are stopped from brushing these experiences aside. These men do not act after the manner of men suffering from an aberration. Out of them has come a great portion of the spiritual wisdom of the race. They are, as it were, among the illuminati of mankind. If "by their fruits ye shall know them," these men have shown fruits so far above the average as to make them spiritual leaders of mankind.

That which occurred to them, and the resultant views of life and the universe which they achieved, must be accepted, then, as authentic enough at least to merit investigation. Keeping in mind also that the average individual is still, in the main, on a lesser plane of development, we shall not be at all surprised if occurrences which take place in those who have apparently, even in a small degree, emerged to a higher level of insight, are regarded as signs, either of supernatural power or of psychic disorder. Is it not possible, on the other hand, to regard these occurrences as signs simply of a higher stage of the very same typical development through which all of us are passing? (Overstreet 1931, p. 239)

Here Overstreet raises an excellent point: Some people regard some of the religious leaders of the world as simply insane; others, as supernaturally influenced. Isn't it possible that they were simply advanced cases of Cosmic Consciousness? This is what Bucke believes.

Considering Emerson's phrase "blasted with an excess of light" —this is also closely related to Bucke's ideas. Buck says that a typical symptom of the onset of Cosmic Consciousness is the experience of intense light—often in the form of "being enveloped in a great flame." Another symptom of Cosmic Consciousness, according to Bucke, is increased personal attractiveness. Now, here is what Emerson says:

The same Omniscence flows into the intellect and makes what we call genius. . . . This energy does not descend into individual life on any other condition than entire possession. It comes to the lowly and simple; it comes to whomsoever will put off what is foreign and proud; it comes as insight; it comes as serenity and grandeur. When we see those whom it inhabits, we are apprised of new degrees of greatness. From that inspiration the man comes back with a changed tone.

Bucke closes his book with the following words:

The simple truth is, that there has lived on the earth, appearing at intervals, for thousands of years among ordinary men, the first faint beginnings of another race; walking the earth and breathing the air with us, but at the same time walking another earth and breathing another air of which we know little or nothing, but which is, all the same, our spiritual life, as its absence would be our spiritual death. This new race is in act of being born from us, and in the near future it will occupy and possess the earth. (Bucke 1956, pp. 383–84)

Well, what are we to make of all this? Is it an idle pipe dream? A reality? A bit of both? Is it the distilled essence of religion? Is it perhaps an inferior substitute? Will we ever know for sure?

I once lent the book to an acquaintance who is a Sanskrit scholar and who is generally into such occult things as astrology. (When I told him that I did not believe in astrology, he replied, "All that means to me is that you have never adequately studied the subject.") Perhaps it is a compliment to the book that he was quite unimpressed by it. As he said to me, "All right, suppose Cosmic Consciousness does come to everyone in time. What will people do then? How will it solve all the social injustices of the world? Just look at all the sickness and poverty and terrorism and child abuse; how will Cosmic Consciousness help all this?"

There are several points to mention. First, he never before had spoken about social problems. Why did he now for the first time? I cannot help but believe that he disliked the idea of Cosmic Consciousness on other grounds (of which he was probably not conscious) and was simply offering an excuse. But the excuse was blatantly ridiculous in view of the fact that both Bucke and Carpenter, who were undoubtedly the main proponents of the idea, saw Cosmic Consciousness and social reform as coming hand in hand. Bucke (who himself had a strong illumination) led an extremely active life and instituted many radical reforms in the treatment of psychiatric patients. And, as I have said, Carpenter was extremely active for the rights of labor and the rights of women. And considering Walt Whitman's voluntary service to wounded soldiers, his Cosmic Consciousness was certainly not unrelated to active social service! However, even if Cosmic Consciousness were totally unrelated to social service and reform, it wouldn't mean that it was without value! Granted that social reform is of major importance, it doesn't follow that it is the *only* thing of great importance. It's the old question of Martha and Mary again. (Martha chose a good part, but Mary chose the better part.)

Another criticism of Bucke is that he didn't sufficiently emphasize the fact that some people must consciously *strive* to obtain Cosmic Consciousness. (Quite frankly, that's one of the features of the book I liked best! Perhaps I am simply the lazy type.) But this raises the interesting question of why some people obtain Cosmic Consciousness without working for it, and others must work for it. Hindus and Buddhists might explain this on the grounds of reincarnation: Those who obtain it in this life without conscious effort have worked for it in previous lives. Who knows?

I wonder how the orthodox religions would react to the idea of Cosmic Consciousness? I would guess that on the whole the Eastern religions would react quite favorably. Indeed, Hinduism is in spirit so much like that of Cosmic Consciousness! I do think Bucke should have included many passages of the Vedanta and the Bhagavad Gita; I cannot imagine Cosmic Consciousness in a more intense form!

I imagine that Orthodox Jews and Moslems would react less favorably, since the personal God, though not actually denied, is certainly not emphasized. What about Christians? Well, I can imagine three different reactions. First, there may be those who would regard the whole thing as from the devil—a diabolically clever *substitute* for religion! Next, there may be those who would say, "Cosmic Consciousness is all right as far as it goes, but it doesn't go far enough; it doesn't emphasize the personal nature of God and His incarnation in Jesus Christ." Then there are those enlightened Christians (at least I would call them enlightened) who would say something like this: "The whole thing is just another name for religion. The Cosmic Consciousness people like Bucke look at the name 'Christ' as just another name for Cosmic Consciousness. By the same token, we can just as well regard 'Cosmic Consciousness' as just another name for being in Christ. And so if the two are really the same, what difference does it make what you call it?"

I *do* wish that religious leaders would state their views on all this. The lack of literature on the subject is appalling!

And now let me conclude on a personal note. Comparing the idea of Cosmic Consciousness with the more orthodox religions, the following thoughts occur to me. Many orthodox Christian sects regard Jesus as an incarnation of God and the *only* incarnation of God. Hindus believe that God (Brahma) has had many incarnations (and I believe *some* Hindus may regard Jesus as being one of them.) Jews and Moslems, of course, believe that God has never had *any* incarnations, and personally, I tend to agree with them on this point (assuming that there is a God). Yet people like Jesus, Mohammed, Buddha, Krishna certainly seem to have *something* very much out of the ordinary! The hypothesis that they were unusually advanced cases of Cosmic Consciousness would strike many as far more plausible than that any of them were *incarnations!* Thus, I find that the Cosmic Consciousness explanation seems more compatible with pure monotheism than the hypothesis of incarnation.

To end on a personal note, what I find particularly attractive about the idea of Cosmic Consciousness is that it seems to be totally free of any sadistic or masochistic tendencies—I cannot find a speck of cruelty in it anywhere. And this is saying a lot! However true or false the various inherent ideas may be, they are surely motivated by pure goodness. I do not believe the ideas are wholly accurate or perfectly formulated as they now stand (as Edward Carpenter said, "I do not think the matter can be defined as yet"), but I agree with Overstreet that of all the religious, mystical, or metaphysical ideas yet proposed, this may well be the most plausible and the most promising.

REFERENCES

Berdyaev, Nicholas. 1950. *Dream and Reality.* London: Geoffrey Bles.
———. 1953. *Truth and Revelation.* London: Geoffrey Bles.
Berkeley, George. 1901. *The Works of George Berkeley.* Vol. IV. Oxford: Clarendon Press.
Bucke, Richard Maurice. 1956. *Cosmic Consciousness.* 18th ed. New York: E. P. Dutton. First published in 1901.
Burroughs, John. 1920. *Accepting the Universe.* Boston: Houghton Mifflin.
Caithness, Marie Sinclair, Countess of. 1876. *Old Truths in a New Light, or, An Earnest Endeavor to Reconcile Material Science with Spiritual Science, and with Scripture.* London: Chapman and Hall.
Carpenter, Edward. 1889. *Civilization: Its Cause and Cure.* London: Swan Sonnenshein.
———. 1892a. *From Adam's Peak to Elephanta.* London: Swan Sonnenshein.
———. 1892b. *Towards Democracy.* 3rd ed. London: T. Fisher Unwin.
Crane, Frank. *Why I Am a Christian.* New York: William Wise, 1924.
Dante. *Purgatory.* 1892. Translated by Charles Eliot Norton. Boston: Houghton Mifflin.
———. *The Divine Comedy.* 1909. Translated by Henry Wadsworth Longfellow. In *The Works of Henry Wadsworth Longfellow,* vol. VIII. Boston: C. T. Brainard.
———. *The Divine Comedy.* 1948. Translated by Lawrence Grant White. New York: Pantheon Books.
Ellis, Havelock. 1923a. *The Dance of Life.* Boston: Houghton Mifflin.
———. 1923b. *Impressions and Comments—First Series.* Boston: Houghton Mifflin.
Frazer, R. W. 1915. *Indian Thought, Past and Present.* London: T. Fisher Unwin.
Freud, Sigmund. 1958. *On Creativity and the Unconscious.* New York: Harper and Brothers.
Gardner, Martin. 1973. *The Flight of Peter Fromm.* Los Altos, Calif.: William Kaufman.
———. *The Whys of a Philosophical Scrivener.* 1983. New York: William Morrow.
Head, J., and S. L. Cranston. 1968. *Reincarnation.* Wheaton, Ill.: Theosophical Publishing House.
Holt, Henry. 1914. *On Cosmic Relations.* Boston: Houghton Mifflin.
Huxley, Aldous. 1945. *The Perennial Philosophy.* New York: Harper & Row.
Kaufman, Walter. 1961. *The Faith of a Heretic.* New York: Doubleday.
Keene, Donald, ed. 1935. *Anthology of Japanese Literature.* New York: Grove Press.

Kushner, Lawrence. 1981. *The River of Light.* Chappaqua, N.Y.: Rossel Books.

Lewis, C. S. 1962. *The Problem of Pain.* London: Fantana Books.

Overstreet, H. A. 1931. *The Enduring Quest.* New York: W. W. Norton.

Peterson, Houston. 1928. *Havelock Ellis: Philosopher of Love.* Boston: Houghton Mifflin.

Russell, Bertrand. 1929. *Mysticism and Logic.* New York: W. W. Norton.

———. 1945. *A History of Western Philosophy.* New York: Simon & Schuster.

Sand, George. 1893. *Convent Life.* Boston: Roberts Brothers.

Suzuki, Daisetz. 1957. *Mysticism: Christian and Buddhist.* New York: Harper & Brothers.

Tennyson, Hallam Lord. 1897. *Alfred Lord Tennyson: A Memoir, by His Son.* 2 vols. London: Macmillan.

That Unknown Country; or, What Living Men Believe Concerning Punishment after Death. 1889. Springfield, Mass.: C. A. Nichols.

Unamuno, Miguel de. 1889. *The Tragic Sense of Life.* Springfield, Mass.: Macmillan.

———. 1925. *Essays and Soliloquies.* New York: Alfred A. Knopf.

Upanishads. 1957. Translated by Swami Prabhavananda and Frederick Manchester. New York: New American Library of World Literature.

Vaughn, Robert Alfred. 1893. *Hours with the Mystics.* 6th ed. 2 vols. New York: Charles Scribner's Sons.

Whitman, Walter. 1885 (1860–61). *Leaves of Grass.* Boston: Thayer and Eldridge.

INDEX

accountability, for injury to others, 49–50

Acklom, George Moreley, 100–101

afterlife: beliefs about, 8, 49–50; communication with dead spirits, 26–27; as dreamless sleep, 15–17; evidence for, 13; false hope about, 30; Freud on, 14; Gardner on, 10, 24; Goethe on, 15; jokes about, 31; Judaism and, 93–94; Kant on, 10; lack of evidence for, 26–27; link with existence of God, 10–12; nature of, 15–16; pantheism and, 12–13; punishment in, 49–50 (*see also* eternal punishment); rationality and belief in, 28–31; reincarnation and, 38, 39–40; as superstition, 4–5; Unamuno on, 23–24; wishful thinking and, 13–14

agnostics and agnosticism: Gardner attitude toward, 7–8; impartiality toward existence of God, 8; as philosophical position, 9; on salvation, 80

Akemi, Tachibama, 110

Alexander, Samuel, 21, 34

angels, lack of free will of, 37

atheists and atheism: on afterlife, 24–25; on existence of God, 8; gap with belief in God, 3; Gardner attitude toward, 7–8; goodness of, 50–51; materialistic vs. idealistic, 25; on nature as God, 19; Shelley on, 21; Smullyan on, 40

Augustine, Saint, 52

Bacon, Francis, 117

Bacon, Leonard, 58

Balzac, Honoré de, 123, 125

Berdyaev, Nicholas, 25, 40, 52

Berkeley, George, 41–43

Bible, fallibility of, 84

Blake, William, 119

born-again Christians, 82–83

Bowsma, Oswald, 34–35

Brahma, 19, 36

Bucke, Richard Maurice: career of, 100; on conversion, 126; on cosmic consciousness, 36, 40, 99–105, 116–117, 131; on Dante, 116; on God as universe, 103; on insanity and cosmic consciousness, 127–128, 130; on Shakespeare, 117–119; on Whitman, 105–106, 110–111, 113; on William Blake, 119

Buddhism: belief in afterlife without belief in God, 11; belief about salvation, 4; cosmic consciousness and, 113; salvation and, 51

Burroughs, John, 49

Caithness, Marie Sinclair (Countess), 39

Calvin, John, 17

Calvinists: on eternal punishment, 64–65; predestination doctrine, 61, 64; on salvation, 69–71

Carpenter, Edward: career of, 120; on cosmic consciousness, 36, 100, 116, 121–123, 134; as social reformer, 120–121

Carroll, Lewis: on eternal punishment, 41; as kind-hearted Christian, 52

Catholicism, 67

Christian Universalism, 4, 38, 49–50

Christians and Christianity: belief in God without belief in afterlife, 11, 49–50; born-again, 82–83; eternal punishment beliefs of, 40–41, 49–50; on salvation, 51; soft vs. hard, 51–53 (*see also* hard Christianity; soft Christianity)

circumstantial evidence, for existence of God, 5

civilization, retributive ethics and, 87

Raymond M. Smullyan, a retired distinguished professor of philosophy, has authored over twenty books. He has had a remarkably diverse sequence of careers—as a pianist, magician, mathematical logician, philosopher, and essayist. His widely known writings are on such varied topics as mathematical logic, retrograde chess analysis, stereo photography, Chinese philosophy, psychology, and religion. He currently resides with his musician wife Blanche in the Catskill Mountains of upper New York State.